— 150 —
BOOKSTORES
YOU NEED
TO VISIT BEFORE
— YOU DIE —

By Elizabeth Stamp

Lannoo

Introduction by Elizabeth Stamp

For as long as I can remember, I have been happiest while wandering the aisles of a bookstore. My small hometown of Wheeling, West Virginia, had two independent bookstores (shoutout to The Paradox Book Store and the late, great Words & Music), and I learned from a young age that bookstores are magical places. As I gathered the bookstores for this book, I began with a very general qualification: Is this a bookstore I'd want to visit? However, since every bookstore is a bookstore I'd want to visit, I had to come up with more specific criteria. There is something special about each bookstore in this book, whether it's wondrous architecture, a highly specialized inventory list or the impact it makes on the community it serves.

In the age of Amazon, bookstores face incredible challenges, which is why it's important to support your local independent bookseller by stopping in, buying from them online, or giving them a call to ask for their expert recommendations. There's a popular saying amongst indie booksellers that I learned at the lovely Indigo Books on Johns Island, South Carolina: "Find it here, buy it here, keep us here." I hope you'll enjoy being transported to these unique stores as much as I have, and that you'll pay them a visit and keep them around for the next generation of book lovers.

Elizabeth Stamp

OVERVIEW

OVERVIEW

01   **BIBLIOTHEK**

2nd floor Unit SY-203, building F3, Arkan Plaza,
Sheikh Zayed City, Giza Governorate 12588, Egypt

TO VISIT
BEFORE YOU DIE
BECAUSE

You can find
your next
read, discover
enlightening art
and caffeinate all
in one stop.

In 2021, Amr Baraka founded Bibliothek, a cultural hub in the Sheikh Zayed area of Cairo designed to serve as a local learning and art destination. The neighborhood spot includes a bookstore, a gallery space and a café, offering the community a place to gather for art exhibits, book readings or conversations over cups of coffee. Visitors can get lost in the aisles while browsing a wide range of titles from classic novels to recent bestsellers, take in the latest exhibition or join the local professionals and students working in the café.

02   CHECHE BOOKS

Kauria Close, Lavington, Nairobi, Kenya

TO VISIT
BEFORE YOU DIE
BECAUSE

The sunny store has a fantastic selection of works by African and diaspora writers.

It's hard not to smile upon stepping inside Cheche Books in the Lavington neighborhood of Nairobi. The cheerful store is filled with bright colors and patterns and mural-decorated walls. Cheche Books opened in 2020 as an independent Pan-African feminist bookstore, café and event space, and the mission of its founder, Ubax Abdi, is to make books by African and diaspora writers more affordable and accessible to local readers. The store also serves as a cultural hub for the community with readings, film screenings, music sessions and exhibitions. Curl up with a good book on the porch beneath the mural of influential women, such as Toni Morrison, Winnie Mandela, Wangari Maathai, Alice Walker and Mariama Bâ.

03   YSL BOOKSHOP

Rue Yves Saint Laurent,
40090 Marrakech, Morocco

TO VISIT
BEFORE YOU DIE
BECAUSE

You'll feel like you're stepping back in time to the designer's Rive Gauche boutique.

Although designer Yves Saint Laurent operated his fashion house in Paris, he had a long love affair with Marrakech. The city is home to Musée Yves Saint Laurent Marrakech and its beautiful YSL Bookshop. The store draws inspiration from the designer's Rive Gauche ready-to-wear boutique, which opened in 1966 with a striking design by architect Isabelle Hebey. Find books related to Morocco, fashion and the designer in this sophisticated space, which features oxblood walls, lacquered displays and lanterns by Isamu Noguchi. The store also stocks books and films that inspired Saint Laurent, such as works by Visconti and Proust.

04 LIBRAIRIE LES INSOLITES

28 Khalid Ibn El Oualid,
Tanger 90000, Morocco

**TO VISIT
BEFORE YOU DIE
BECAUSE**

You can find
intriguing books
and art in the
bookstore-slash-
gallery.

Founded over 12 years ago by writer Stéphanie Gaou, Librairie les Insolites is a charming bookstore and art gallery in Tangier. Les Insolites translates to "the unusuals," and that's what shoppers can expect to find on the store's walls and its sunny yellow shelves. Customers can browse books, stationery and the latest exhibit of paintings, photography or sculpture, then spend some time soaking up the Moroccan sun and diving into the pages of their purchases at the café tables outside the store. Younger readers will also find plenty to love in the kids and young adult section. If you can't make it to the store in person, you can still experience the Tangier literary scene by listening to its podcast, Radio les Insolites.

05 JAZZHOLE

168 Awolowo Road, Ikoyi 106104,
Lagos, Nigeria

This beloved store is a must-visit for music fans on the hunt for books and vinyl.

A Lagos institution, Jazzhole is a destination for book and music lovers alike. Owner Kunle Tejuoso, whose mother is the founder of the city's Glendora Bookshop chain, opened the store in 1991, and since then it has become a landmark that counts Lagos local and author Chimamanda Ngozi Adichie—who name-checked the store in her book *Americanah*—amongst its fans. The one-room space is part bookstore, part record shop, and part performance space where customers can enjoy live music, browse the impressive selection of books, CDs and rare vinyl and enjoy a cup of coffee in the café area.

06 CLARKE'S BOOKSHOP

199 Long Street,
Cape Town 8001, South Africa

TO VISIT
BEFORE YOU DIE
BECAUSE

The store has a wealth of titles on Africa, particularly Southern Africa.

Since it was founded in 1957 by Anthony Clarke, the bookstore has become a staple on Long Street in the center of Cape Town. Clarke's began as a secondhand bookstore, but its inventory has since expanded to include new titles, maps, collectable books and prints. In the 1970s, the store began specializing in books on Africa, especially Southern Africa, and Clarke's is now a destination for shoppers and libraries interested in books on the region's history, art and literature. Customers can climb the stairs to visit the Africana room and a room dedicated to secondhand books that harks back to the store's early years.

07   KALK BAY BOOKS

62 Main Road, Kalk Bay,
Cape Town 7975, South Africa

TO VISIT
BEFORE YOU DIE
BECAUSE

This charming seaside store is an ideal place to while away the afternoon.

Kalk Bay Books is a small independent store set in the seaside village of Kalk Bay in Cape Town. It opened in 2006 and moved to its current location in the "Orange Building" in 2020. The welcoming, homey store is the kind of place where you can stay a while, curl up with a book on a comfy sofa and get lost in the pages. While you don't even need to go inside for a bit of enlightenment—thanks to the chalkboard out front that's updated with intriguing quotes—you definitely should take the time to browse or to tickle the ivories on the piano by the door.

08   **BRIDGE BOOKS**

8 Commissioner Street, Marshalltown,
Johannesburg 2001, South Africa

TO VISIT
BEFORE YOU DIE
BECAUSE

The store offers
the opportunity to
immerse yourself
in Johannesburg's
book-filled
history.

In 2016, journalist-turned-bookseller Griffin Shea opened Bridge
Books, a store specializing in African literature, in the heart of
Johannesburg. Customers can browse three floors of handpicked
new and secondhand books, and in the children's section younger
readers can find stories in all of South Africa's 11 languages. Be sure
to make a reservation for the store's guided walking tours of underground booksellers, which give participants a look at the area's literary legacy and impressive number of booksellers. Aspiring authors
can check out the store's writing and publishing workshops in the
hope of one day seeing their work on Bridge Books' shelves.

09 QUAGGA RARE BOOKS & ART

84/86 Main Road, Kalk Bay, Cape Town 7975, South Africa

TO VISIT
BEFORE YOU DIE
BECAUSE

Stepping inside is like entering a cabinet of curiosities filled with treasures to discover.

With its scarlet red walls and glass cases full of precious and sometimes odd objects, Quagga Rare Books & Art in Kalk Bay is a collector's paradise. Quagga was founded over 25 years ago by George Curtis, who now runs the store with his son Simon, and boasts an eclectic selection of books, maps, prints and art. Book lovers will find first editions and rare volumes on everything from poetry to anthropology and maritime history, while art aficionados will delight in unique lithographs, etchings and paintings. Browse under the watchful eye of a mounted zebra (a relative of the store's namesake species) and peer inside displays of natural and historical artifacts.

10 STELLENBOSCH BOOKS

14 Andringa Street, Stellenbosch 7600, South Africa

Stellenbosch Books feels like a home away from home.

The storefront at 14 Andringa Street has been home to a bookstore since 1959, and in 2020, Stellenbosch Books became the latest purveyor to occupy the space and continue its literary legacy. The plant-filled store feels like a home away from home, thanks to the stylish seating areas—with custom-made furniture and vintage accents—and a friendly staff who will whip you up a cappuccino while you shop. The soundtrack of vinyl records adds to the homey feel and you're encouraged to linger and browse the selection of books, accessories and gifts to your heart's content.

stellenboschbooks.co.za   +27 21 882 6754

11 JAMES FINDLAY COLLECTABLE BOOKS & ANTIQUE MAPS

Rand Club, 33 Loveday Street, Marshalltown,
Johannesburg 2107, South Africa

TO VISIT
BEFORE YOU DIE
BECAUSE

This store, in the basement of the historic Rand Club, is a trove of unique books and objects.

Dealer James Findlay has been selling rare books, maps and art since 1997. In 2018, he opened James Findlay Collectable Books & Antique Maps in the basement of the Rand Club, a private members club in Johannesburg. The over 1800 square-foot location is a combination of bookstore and gallery, complete with a stage for lectures, fairs and other events. Find unique maps and globes, vintage posters, as well as unexpected finds—such as antique tea tins and a Victorian cast-iron book press—alongside beautiful leather-bound books. The store is open by appointment only so be sure to call in advance.

12   A NOVEL IDEA

The Slipway, Shop N°4, Msasani Peninsula,
Dar es salaam, Tanzania

You can browse
15,000 books and
then take in views
of the nearby
Indian Ocean.

Owners Sarah and Paul Clithero opened the first branch of A Novel Idea in Dar es Salaam in 1992, occupying a repurposed 20-foot-long shipping container outfitted with a thatched roof. Local readers quickly embraced the store, and the couple eventually moved into their flagship, a bright and airy spot on the Msasani Peninsula. Over 15,000 titles are spread over the two-story space, displayed on the shelves alongside stationery, imported and locally made gifts, and art supplies. Travelers stopping in Arusha on their way to Mt. Kilimanjaro or a safari can find a branch of A Novel Idea in the city's TFA Center.

13   EL ATENEO GRAND SPLENDID

Avenue Santa Fe 1860, C1123 CABA, Argentina

This epic bookstore is a beautiful reminder of a bygone era of Buenos Aires.

It's no wonder that El Ateneo Grand Splendid in Buenos Aires' Recoleta neighborhood has repeatedly been named one of the world's most beautiful bookstores. The massive store is located in the former Grand Splendid theater, which was built in 1919 by architects Peró and Torres Armengol and once hosted ballet, opera and movies. Peruse the shelves that line the floor and the old luxury boxes, which offer stellar views of the historic space. And if you've dreamed of life beneath the bright lights of Broadway, you can make that a reality with a visit to the café located on the former stage.

14   LIBROS DEL PASAJE

Thames 1762, Palermo,
Buenos Aires C1414DDJ, Argentina

TO VISIT
BEFORE YOU DIE
BECAUSE

This stylish bookstore in trendy Palermo Soho is a happening spot where you can browse and hang out.

In Buenos Aires' fashionable Palermo Soho district, you'll find Libros del Pasaje, a stylish bookstore that's been operating in the city since 2004. The store prides itself on having a comprehensive, ever-changing catalog and an expert staff to help shoppers navigate it. The hip bookstore's home is in an old building with vaulted ceilings and sky-high bookshelves, where you can find everything from bestsellers to volumes from small publishers and imported books. There's always something going on at Libros del Pasaje, whether it's art and photo exhibitions, lectures, book launches or activities for kids, and shoppers can hang out at the café and bar.

15   OLIVA LIBROS

Entre Ríos 579, 2000 Rosario, Santa Fe, Argentina

TO VISIT
BEFORE YOU DIE
BECAUSE

You can explore
Oliva Libros'
stunning space
for hours.

Located on the street level of a spectacular 1915 building known as La Casa de los Dragones, Oliva Libros in Rosario is a bookstore that you can explore for hours. The soaring space blends historical elements, such as a wood mezzanine and grand chandeliers, with industrial touches, including exposed brick walls and stainless steel lights. The spacious store is filled with a variety of books, from classics to poetry and manga. Oliva Libros also hosts regular events in its roomy store including well-attended poetry readings, live music and conversations with authors.

16   LIVRARIA DA TRAVESSA

Rua Visconde de Pirajá 572, Ipanema,
Rio de Janeiro 22410-002, Brazil

TO VISIT
BEFORE YOU DIE
BECAUSE

Take a break
from the beach
and spend
the afternoon
browsing almost
11,000 square feet
of books.

Livraria Da Travessa has its roots in Ipanema, so it's no surprise that even though the brand has grown to include international outposts, it maintains a presence in the fashionable beach neighborhood south of Rio. In 2002, the store opened in a lovely location designed by Bel Lobo/Bob Neri Arquitetura with an open mezzanine overlooking the main shopping area and green-and-white tile floors that give the space a vintage feel. The store is home to nearly 11,000 square feet of books, music, movies and stationery, as well as a mezzanine-level restaurant where you can get everything from coffee to a full meal.

17 LIBRAIRIE DRAWN & QUARTERLY

211 Rue Bernard Ouest, Montréal, QC H2T 2K5, Canada

TO VISIT
BEFORE YOU DIE
BECAUSE

It's heaven on earth for comic and graphic novel lovers.

In 2007, comics publisher Drawn & Quarterly opened their first brick-and-mortar storefront in an old dress store in the Mile End neighborhood of Montréal. Fans of graphic novels will feel like they're in heaven while browsing the world-class collection of comics and graphic novels, including the publisher's own titles, in the cozy and eclectic space. Younger readers will want to check out La Petite Librairie Drawn & Quarterly at 176 Rue Bernard Ouest, which is also where the store hosts its multiple book clubs and events, such as book launches, story hours and an afternoon drawing club.

mtl.drawnandquarterly.com 514-279-2224

18   L'EUGUÉLIONNE

1426 Beaudry, Montréal, Quebec H2L 3E5, Canada

TO VISIT
BEFORE YOU DIE
BECAUSE

L'Euguélionne
is a welcoming
space for feminist
communities and
book lovers.

Named after the 1976 novel by Lucile Durand (published under the nom de plume Louky Bersianik), L'Euguélionne is a feminist bookstore and non-profit solidarity co-op in Montréal. The store was founded in 2016 by a collective of scholars, booksellers and writers, and offers a diverse and intersectional selection of feminist, LGBTQIA2S+, anti-racist and anti-colonial titles. You'll find everything from fiction and history books to comic books and poetry in this inviting store, which also hosts workshops, book launches and discussion groups. Parents can shop stereotype-challenging children's books and YA novels for their future feminists.

19   MUNRO'S BOOKS

1108 Government Street,
Victoria BC V8W 1Y2, Canada

TO VISIT
BEFORE YOU DIE
BECAUSE

The sixty-year-old store set in a heritage bank building is a Victoria landmark.

Founded in 1963 by Jim Munro and his first wife, the Nobel-Prize–winning writer Alice Munro, Munro's Books is a Victoria institution. In 1984, it moved into its current home, a beautifully restored neo-classical bank built in 1909 by architect Thomas Hooper. Browse beneath the 24-foot ceilings and don't miss the fabric works by artist Carole Sabiston depicting the four seasons and classic works of literature that hang on the walls. The knowledgeable and long-serving staff can help you find the perfect title from the broad selection of books in both English and French.

20   QUEEN BOOKS

914 Queen Street East, Toronto, Ontario M4M 1J5, Canada

With a great selection and homey interiors, it's the ideal neighborhood bookstore.

Queen Books in the Leslieville area of Toronto is everything you want in an independent neighborhood bookstore. Founded in 2017 by booksellers Alex Snyder and Liz Burns, the sunny store is a great spot to find picks for your TBR pile, and it offers a wide variety of titles, including works by local authors and a huge kids' section for tiny readers. The store's chic interiors—including vivid wallpaper, pressed tin ceilings and vintage furnishings and rugs—might just inspire you to spruce up your home reading area. And for voracious readers, Queen Books offers subscriptions, allowing you to receive a hand-picked book each month for six months or a year.

21 LIBRERÍA ULISES LASTARRIA

José Victorino Lastarria 70, local 2,
Paseo Barrio Lastarria, Santiago, Chile

Its mirrored ceilings make you feel like you're in an endless cave of books.

Librería Ulises Lastarria opened in the historic and artsy Lastarria neighborhood of Santiago in 2010 and is now a local destination for book lovers. Named for the book by James Joyce and the hero of Homer's epic poem *The Odyssey*, the store feels warm and welcoming thanks to its orange walls and wood furnishings, while mirrored ceilings make the already-tall stacks feel like they go on forever. The store hosts book launches and cultural activities, and its attentive staff are on hand to help customers with the catalog of literature, humanities and social science titles.

22   9 3/4 BOOKSTORE + CAFÉ

Vía Las Palmas, Kilómetro 15 + 750, Envigado, Antioquia, Colombia

TO VISIT
BEFORE YOU DIE
BECAUSE

This whimsical store will delight book lovers, young and old.

Harry Potter stepped into the wizarding world at Platform 9 ¾, and readers of all ages will also find themselves transported upon entering 9 ¾ Bookstore + Café in Antioquia. The charming store is full of whimsical elements, from books suspended from the ceiling—as though they are flying—to walls of lush greenery and rainbow-colored displays. The store offers plenty of family-friendly activities, and there's plenty of comfy seating so you or your kiddos can curl up with a good book and a marshmallow-laden hot chocolate from the café.

23   LIBRERÍA WILBORADA 1047

Calle 71 # 10 47, Bogotá, Colombia

The blend of historical architecture and modern elements creates a unique shopping experience.

Founder Yolanda Auza took inspiration for the name of her Bogatá bookstore from Wiborada, the patron saint of libraries and librarians, who was canonized in 1047. The store is located in a timber-framed 1943 building and offers over 3,000 square feet of space to explore. The interior maintains historical elements contrasted with modern details, such as the steel mesh bridges that cross over the exposed beams, giving shoppers a view of the space below. Grab a drink at Café Cultor and spend the afternoon reading on the patio or in one of the cozy reading areas.

24   CUBA LIBRO

Calle 24, corner Calle 19, Vedado, Havana, Cuba

TO VISIT
BEFORE YOU DIE
BECAUSE

You can grab a book and while the day away reading in one of the lush garden's hammocks.

Cuba Libro is a literary haven in the Vedado district of Havana. The store is the island's first English-language bookstore and café, and since it opened in 2013 it has been a destination for locals and travelers looking to find a book, grab a coffee and hopefully bag a hammock in the garden where they can enjoy both. Cuba Libro offers free events and community workshops and prides itself on being an ethically and socially responsible business and a cultural center for the community. Stop in to browse English books and magazines and sip on one of the café's signature drinks, or a classic café con leche.

25   LA INCREÍBLE

Amsterdam 264, Hipódromo Condesa,
06100 Ciudad de México, Mexico

TO VISIT
BEFORE YOU DIE
BECAUSE

It lives up to
its name as an
incredible spot for
design books.

La increíble is a treasure chest for design lovers in the beautiful La Condesa neighborhood of Mexico City. Founded by graphic designer Alejandro Magallanes and publisher and curator Selva Hernández, the minimalist store is lined with pale wood bookcases from floor to ceiling, and a large center table displays prints and other objects, including collaborations with notable designers. While its main focus is design, you'll also find everything from essays to cookbooks on the shelves. La increíble hosts poetry open mics for emerging poets and book sessions with authors, and even has a podcast, Tumulto, featuring interviews with creatives.

26 CAFEBRERÍA EL PÉNDULO SAN ÁNGEL

Avenida Revolución 1500, Guadalupe Inn, 01020 Ciudad de México, Mexico

The multi-level, nature-filled store has thousands of square feet to explore.

Cafebrería el Péndulo introduced its first café-slash-bookstore in 1993 and currently has seven branches in Mexico City. Its latest location in the San Ángel neighborhood is a modern, airy space filled with books and areas to explore. Architect Eduardo Aizenman turned the cavernous 10,500-square-foot interior with a 26-foot high ceiling into a bustling multi-level store, taking inspiration from the theater next door by creating multiple "stages" within the building, including living room areas and a restaurant. The building is designed around an ash tree and a towering palm, and the suspended planters and wood elements make the store a contemporary yet calming space to shop.

27 THE LAST BOOKSTORE

453 South Spring Street, Los Angeles, CA 90013, USA

TO VISIT
BEFORE YOU DIE
BECAUSE

The book installations are a feast for the eyes—and Instagram.

The Last Bookstore in Downtown L.A. packs plenty of book-themed delights into its 22,000-square-foot location in a former bank building. Founded by owner Josh Spencer in 2005, the business has grown to become California's largest new and used book and record store, with over 250,000 books spread across two floors. Visitors can browse true crime selections on display in an old vault; indulge their artsy side in an annex filled with rare art, architecture and photography volumes; or snap photos in the Instagram-famous book tunnel. The maze-like upper level is the perfect place to get lost for a few hours discovering new titles. Just be sure to bring your camera as surprises await around every corner.

lastbookstorela.com 213-488-0599

28   BOOKS ARE MAGIC

225 Smith Street, Brooklyn, NY 11231, USA

Owners Emma Straub and Michael Fusco-Straub have created a magical and inclusive neighborhood spot.

On a corner of charming Smith Street in Brooklyn's Carroll Gardens is Books Are Magic, a truly enchanting store and the brainchild of bestselling novelist Emma Straub and designer Michael Fusco-Straub. The warm and welcoming spot is packed with carefully curated selections, and the sizable children's section is brimming with delightful finds for the neighborhood's many curious young readers. Books are Magic hosts frequent events showcasing up-and-coming authors and beloved writers and it recently expanded to a second location in nearby Brooklyn Heights. Find a new favorite read, then commemorate your visit with a selfie in front of the much-Instagrammed mural outside.

booksaremagic.net   718-246-2665

29   THE STRAND

828 Broadway, New York, NY 10003, USA

TO VISIT
BEFORE YOU DIE
BECAUSE

Browse 18 miles
of books in
New York City's
most popular
and beloved
independent
bookstore.

You can't walk a block in New York City without seeing some-
one carrying a tote bag from The Strand. Founded by Ben Bass
in 1927, The Strand has been a New York institution for over 95
years. The sprawling flagship is home to over 2.5 million new, used
and rare books, including those on the legendary dollar carts outside the store. The store is now run by the third generation of Bass
booksellers and has expanded to include stores on the Upper West
Side, LaGuardia Airport and a kiosk in Central Park. But it's this
Greenwich Village location that can't be missed.

30   **RIZZOLI**

1133 Broadway, New York, NY 10010, USA

Known for its volumes on architecture, design, art, fashion and cooking, Rizzoli has been selling books in New York City since 1964. The store has been located in the St. James Building in the city's NoMad neighborhood since 2015, and the space's black-and-white marble floors, towering columns, brass chandeliers and whimsical wallpaper allow shoppers to feel transported. Check out its legendary window installations on your way in, then take your time browsing the beautifully illustrated titles. If your shelves at home are a bit bare, Rizzoli will curate a custom-made library for you, or you can sign up for a subscription to have new books delivered monthly.

31 CITY LIGHTS BOOKSTORE

261 Columbus Avenue, San Francisco, CA 94133, USA

TO VISIT
BEFORE YOU DIE
BECAUSE

This San
Francisco
store holds an
important place
in literary and
cultural history.

A counterculture landmark, City Lights is a San Francisco institution with a rich history as the cultural hub of the Beat Generation, a beloved bookstore and an influential publisher of such works as Allen Ginsberg's *Howl*. Founded in 1953 by poet Lawrence Ferlinghetti and professor Peter D. Martin, the store was the U.S.'s first all-paperback bookstore, initially focusing on modern literature and works on progressive politics. It has expanded quite a bit over the years and now includes three floors of hardcovers and paperbacks from major publishers and small imprints alike. The store's original progressive spirit lives on through its selections and its foundation.

        citylights.com   415-362-8193

32 POWELL'S BOOKS

1005 West Burnside Street, Portland, OR 97209, USA

It's the world's largest independent bookstore.

The flagship store of Powell's Books in Portland, Oregon, is called the City of Books for a reason. Open 365 days a year, Powell's City of Books is the world's largest new and used bookstore, occupying a city block and housing over one million books in its nine color-coded rooms. Spend an afternoon (or an entire weekend!) browsing the 3,500 different sections, or stop in the elegant 1,000-square-foot Rare Books Room to check out first editions and antiquarian books. The family business is now in its third generation and has two additional locations in Portland.

33 FULTON STREET BOOKS & COFFEE

210 West Latimer Street, Tulsa, OK 74106, USA

TO VISIT
BEFORE YOU DIE
BECAUSE

This inclusive space is making a difference in the community.

Onikah Asamoa-Caesar had a clear mission when she founded Fulton Street Books & Coffee in Tulsa, Oklahoma: create community, promote literacy and increase representation. The welcoming store centers books and stories often overlooked by major chains, and 70% of its titles are written by or feature people of color or marginalized communities. The store also hosts frequent events and community programs, including Fatherhood Fridays, a reading time for dads and kids, and Noise on Fulton Street, the store's take on NPR's Tiny Desk series. The café is the perfect spot to relax with a new book and a seasonal drink and pastry.

34   BART'S BOOKS

302 West Matilija Street, Ojai, CA 93023, USA

While some stores may claim to have everything under the sun, Bart's Books in Ojai, California, prides itself on actually having everything... under the sun. The outdoor bookstore began in 1964 as a set of bookcases outside the home of founder Richard Bartinsdale, who was inspired by the Bouquinistes of Paris. Today the scenic store is home to nearly a million books, including 35-cent volumes that line the exterior walls and can be purchased by putting money through a slot in the door. While most of the books are secondhand, Barts also stocks some new titles, rare books and staff picks.

35 ARCANA: BOOKS ON THE ARTS

8675 Washington Boulevard, Culver City, CA 90232, USA

TO VISIT
BEFORE YOU DIE
BECAUSE

The industrial space is home to 100,000 new and rare art books.

Arcana: Books on the Arts has been selling new, rare and out-of-print books in Culver City for almost 40 years. The business is currently located in the Helms Bakery District in a bright and expansive gallery-like space. Owners Whitney and Lee Kaplan have over 100,000 items in stock, including a mix of books, catalogs and ephemera related to 20th- and 21st-century art, design, architecture and fashion. Art fans should keep an eye on Arcana's events calendar, which includes signings and conversations with noteworthy artists and authors.

arcanabooks.com 310-458-1499

36   ALBERTINE

972 Fifth Avenue, New York, NY 10075, USA

TO VISIT
BEFORE YOU DIE
BECAUSE

There's no better spot in the U.S. to find literature and magazines from French-speaking countries.

A project of the Cultural Services of the French Embassy, Albertine is a bookstore dedicated to French–American intellectual exchange. The elegant store opened in 2014 in the historic Stanford White-designed Payne Whitney mansion in a stunning space created by famed French designer Jacques Garcia. Browse over 14,000 French and English titles from 30 French-speaking countries beneath the hand-painted ceiling, which features a celestial mural inspired by a ceiling at the Villa Stuck in Munich. Busts of influential figures in French and French–American history, such as René Descartes, Benjamin Franklin and Alexis de Tocqueville, add to the atmosphere, along with a replica of Michelangelo's *Young Archer* on loan from the Metropolitan Museum of Art.

37 ARUNDEL BOOKS

322 1st Avenue S., Seattle, WA 98104, USA

TO VISIT
BEFORE YOU DIE
BECAUSE

You can find
an excellent
selection of new
and rare books in
a lovely historic
setting.

Arundel Books began as a publisher of art and poetry in 1984, and has grown and evolved over the years to now include a number of operations, including a bookstore in Seattle. In 2021, the store moved to its current Pioneer Square location, which boasts incredible friezes and vaulted ceilings. Booklovers can find a diverse list of titles from history to sci-fi, as well as a curated inventory of rare books in a variety of genres, including literature, philosophy and the Pacific Northwest. True to its original mission, you can still find an exceptional selection of art and poetry books.

arundelbooks.com 206-624-4442

38 THE MYSTERIOUS BOOKSHOP

58 Warren Street, New York, NY 10007, USA

TO VISIT
BEFORE YOU DIE
BECAUSE

It's heaven on earth for mystery lovers.

The Mysterious Bookshop has been delighting lovers of whodunits since Otto Penzler opened the store in 1979. Now located in Tribeca, it is the oldest mystery specialist store in America with something to offer every crime lover, whether they're into espionage, thrillers or suspense. Find shelves upon shelves of page turners, including first editions, rare books and Sherlockiana. Bookstore enthusiasts won't want to miss its Bibliomystery Series, a collection of novellas about books, libraries, bookstores and collectors. If you want to build out your home library, subscribe to one of the store's ten crime clubs and have a signed first edition of your chosen genre of mystery delivered to your door every month.

mysteriousbookshop.com   212-587-1011

39   SQUARE BOOKS

160 Courthouse Square, Oxford, MS 38655, USA

TO VISIT
BEFORE YOU DIE
BECAUSE

This legendary bookstore in Oxford, Mississippi, is adored by generations of writers.

Square Books is not just a local landmark but a literary one too. Located in the historic town square of Oxford since it was founded in 1979, Square Books now has four stores in three buildings that include a children's bookstore, a store with lifestyle and leisure titles and an outpost with rare and collectible books. Over the years, Square Books has become a beloved spot for the community and the thousands of writers who have visited the store and been embraced by its owners, the Howorth family, who in the past would house authors in their guest room. Peruse the excellent selection of literary fiction or pick up a book by Oxford's own William Faulkner.

40 SKYLARK BOOKSHOP

22 South 9th Street, Columbia, MO 65201, USA

TO VISIT
BEFORE YOU DIE
BECAUSE

Skylark Bookshop
is helping to
make Columbia,
Missouri,
a literary
destination.

Novelist Alex George has helped turn Columbia, Missouri, into a destination for writers and readers with the Unbound Literary Festival, which he founded in 2016, and Skylark Bookshop, which followed in 2018. The small but lovely bookshop stocks an expertly curated selection of titles in a beautiful space complete with elegant moldings and a vaulted ceiling. Skylark is a community hub, hosting its monthly Skylarking Book Club and various events from book signings to drag queen story times, and the booksellers encourage customers to bring their dogs to the shop with them. If you need another reason to visit, just look to the shop's simple but apt motto: "Because Books."

41   BRATTLE BOOK SHOP

9 West Street, Boston, MA 02111, USA

TO VISIT
BEFORE YOU DIE
BECAUSE

You never know
what delights
you'll find in the
outdoor book lot.

Established in 1825, Brattle Book Shop in downtown Boston is one of the oldest and largest antiquarian bookstores in the U.S. Its three-story location is home to over 250,000 used books, as well as maps, prints and other ephemera, and collectors will find treasures such as first editions and leather-bound books in the rare book room. Brattle is famous for its outdoor book lot next to the building, where rows of carts and shelves hold used books at bargain prices. The Gloss family has operated the store since 1949, and bookseller Kenneth Gloss can be heard on the store's podcast, Brattlecast: A Firsthand Look at Secondhand Books.

42 THE BOOK BARN

41 West Main Street, Niantic, CT 06357, USA

You can browse 500,000 books and meet some friendly goats at this one-of-a-kind bookstore.

Established in 1988, The Book Barn in Niantic, Connecticut, is heaven for book lovers. The sprawling complex is home to the Main Barn, with three levels of books, multiple themed buildings and outdoor shopping areas. Visitors can find over half a million used books across the property—even in the former outhouse—as well as plenty of cats and even some goats. Find dollar books in "Hades," a makeshift building with assorted books, browse new arrivals at the "Ellis Island" stands, or peruse poetry and leather-bound titles in "The Haunted," a two-story building behind the garden. The Book Barn is a one-of-a-kind shopping experience where you're sure to find surprises (or a cat) around every corner.

bookbarnniantic.com   860-739-5715

43 THE BOOKSTORE AT OXFORD EXCHANGE

420 West Kennedy Boulevard, Tampa, FL 33606, USA

TO VISIT
BEFORE YOU DIE
BECAUSE

The unconventional book displays will lead you to unexpected finds.

Oxford Exchange in Tampa has plenty of attractions, including a restaurant, a workspace and a retail store, but perhaps its biggest draw is The Bookstore, offering a well-curated selection in a stunning English-inspired space. Many of the books are grouped by theme, allowing customers to find books they might have overlooked otherwise, and the store sells beautiful versions of classic titles, including their OE Library Collection, a modern take on leatherbound books. The Bookstore also offers subscriptions and will send readers signed new releases monthly for six months or a year.

44   BOOKS & BOOKS

265 Aragon Avenue, Coral Gables, FL 33134, USA

TO VISIT
BEFORE YOU DIE
BECAUSE

Books & Books in Coral Gables is a South Florida landmark.

Books & Books was founded by Mitchell Kaplan in 1982, and since then it has grown into one of the best independent bookstores in the country, with multiple branches in South Florida. The Coral Gables location is a must-visit, partly because of its spectacular setting. The store is located in a gorgeous 9,000-square-foot Mediterranean-style building from 1927. The interior offers a beautiful place to browse, with high ceilings, a fireplace, original tile floors, and tall, dark wood bookcases. Customers can also enjoy the open-air courtyard and café and find a large selection of national and international papers and magazines in the newsstand outside.

45 NEW DOMINION BOOKSHOP

404 East Main Street, Charlottesville, VA 22902, USA

TO VISIT
BEFORE YOU DIE
BECAUSE

It's the oldest independent bookstore in Virginia and boasts a secret garden.

Venture to Charlottesville's bustling Downtown Mall to find New Dominion Bookshop, the commonwealth's oldest independent book-store. The shop opened in 1924 and has long been a favorite of locals and visiting authors alike, including its most famous customer, William Faulkner, who visited while serving as a writer-in-residence at the University of Virginia in the late 1950s. It's been in its East Main Street home since 1990 and offers a wonderfully curated list of new fiction, non-fiction and community titles. It's worth planning a visit in the spring so you can fully enjoy the elegant rose garden with bloom-covered trellises tucked away behind the shop.

46 SEMICOLON

515 North Halsted Street,
Chicago, IL 60642, USA

TO VISIT
BEFORE YOU DIE
BECAUSE

Semicolon
celebrates authors
of color and local
street artists.

Danielle Mullen opened Chicago's Semicolon Bookstore + Gallery in 2019 with a focus on showcasing books by authors of color and work by local street artists. Colorful murals line the walls of the River West area store, which also boasts plenty of cozy seating areas. Semicolon hosts frequent author events, and in 2022 it hosted its first Lit Fest, a book-fueled bash that took over two city blocks. The store is also home to the literacy-focused nonprofit Parenthesis, whose mission is to close the literacy gap in marginalized communities. Parenthesis supports the store's #ClearTheShelves initiative to give away books to local students.

47 EXILE IN BOOKVILLE

410 South Michigan Avenue, Suite 210, Chicago, IL 60605, USA

TO VISIT
BEFORE YOU DIE
BECAUSE

This small store in the Fine Arts Building is a great place to be exiled for an afternoon.

Exile in Bookville is a store that believes books and music are synonymous, hence its name—a wink to Liz Phair's 1993 classic album *Exile in Guyville*—and its stock, which blends literature and vinyl. Owners Javier Ramirez and Kristin Enola Gilbert initially started Exile in Bookville as an online store, and in 2021 they took over a second-floor space—formerly home to used bookstore Dial Books— in the historic Fine Arts Building on Michigan Avenue. They've made the store their own, bringing in new books and filling the floor-to-ceiling shelves with their expert selections of literature from both major publishers and small presses.

exileinbookville.com 312-753-3154

48   E. SHAVER, BOOKSELLER

326 Bull Street, Savannah, GA 31401, USA

TO VISIT
BEFORE YOU DIE
BECAUSE

The cat-filled
bookstore is a
community hub in
a historic home.

E. Shaver, Bookseller has been serving the Savannah community since 1975, when newlyweds Ed and Ester Shaver visited the city on their honeymoon and decided to put down roots and open a bookstore. E. Shaver is now owned by Jessica Osborne and Melissa Taylor, who continue to operate the store out of an 1842 building, which was originally built by female builder Eliza Jewett as her home. Local readers can join one of the store's themed book clubs, focusing on everything from poetry to graphic novels and Jane Austen. Stop in to peruse the shelves and to meet Bartleby, Mr. Eliot, Skimbleshanks and Morticia, the bookstore cats.

49 KRAMERS

1517 Connecticut Avenue NW, Washington, D.C. 20036, USA

Kramers has been a D.C. institution since 1976.

If you're a bibliophile looking for a gathering space in Washington, D.C., look no further than Kramers in Dupont Circle. The store, formerly known as Kramerbooks, opened in 1976 as the first bookstore/café in the nation's capital. Over the years this neighborhood fixture has hosted its fair share of political and literary elites and continues to offer a variety of events, including book readings, conversations with authors, comedy shows, trivia nights and live music. The café has grown into a restaurant and bar offering all-day dining and cocktails. If you're in D.C. and find yourself with a book emergency, Kramers will deliver locally within an hour.

kramers.com   202-387-1400

50 UNDER THE UMBRELLA

511 W. 200 S., Suite 120, Salt Lake City, UT 84101, USA

TO VISIT
BEFORE YOU DIE
BECAUSE

Under the Umbrella celebrates queer authors and queer stories in a welcoming space.

Under the Umbrella describes itself as a queer little bookstore, but the space is much more than a place to buy books; it's a hub for the 2SLGBTQIA+ community in Salt Lake City. The store carries books of all genres for readers of all ages, either by queer authors or with a queer focus, in a vibrant and airy space decorated with murals and a gallery showcasing local artists. Under the Umbrella also opens its doors for a variety of regular and special events, including daily coworking, monthly book clubs, tarot card readings and book-themed speed dating.

undertheumbrellabookstore.com 801-922-0923

51 FAULKNER HOUSE BOOKS

624 Pirate's Alley, New Orleans, LA 70116, USA

TO VISIT
BEFORE YOU DIE
BECAUSE

The historic store was the former home of William Faulkner and a literary landmark in its own right.

Stroll down the picturesque Pirate's Alley in the French Quarter to reach the blue-shuttered doors of Faulkner House Books. The 1837 building's most famous resident, William Faulkner, lived on the first floor in the 1920s while writing his first novel, *Soldier's Pay*. In 1988 Joseph J. DeSalvo Jr. and Rosemary James opened the small bookstore, which has become a "Crescent City" landmark in its own right. The charming store features elegant wood furnishings, such as tables piled with books and glass-front secretaries which hold rare editions. Stop by to take in the historical atmosphere and pick up a book by the store's namesake or allow the well-read staff to recommend the ideal title.

faulknerhousebooks.com 504-524-2940

52   M. JUDSON BOOKSELLERS

130 South Main Street, Suite 200A, Greenville, SC 29601, USA

TO VISIT BEFORE YOU DIE BECAUSE

This independent Greenville bookstore offers everything from a restaurant to vintage furniture in addition to plenty of good books.

M. Judson Booksellers has been serving the community of Greenville, South Carolina, since 2015, when it opened in a historic courthouse downtown. Named for Mary Camilla Judson, a 19th-century educator in Greenville, the store is a welcoming space for story lovers, complete with a full-service restaurant, Camilla Kitchen, a 4th-floor event space and a selection of vintage furnishings so you can recreate the feel of the store at home. The store offers Letterbox, a thematic or custom-made monthly book subscription service that will deliver books to your doorstep. If you're local, M. Judson offers book clubs for every reader, whether you're interested in Southern literature or sci-fi.

53 THE CENTER FOR FICTION BOOKSTORE

15 Lafayette Avenue, Brooklyn, NY 11217, USA

**TO VISIT
BEFORE YOU DIE
BECAUSE**

The 200-year-old organization's latest act includes a captivating bookstore.

The Center for Fiction began over 200 years ago as the Mercantile Library of New York, and today the literary non-profit operates out of a vibrant Brooklyn home, which includes an independent bookstore, a café and bar and a members-only library. Find everything from bestsellers to hard-to-find titles in the spectacular space featuring soaring bookcases, alcoves displaying busts of famous authors and café tables inscribed with literary quotes. The Center is also renowned for its literary events, which include discussions with famed authors, wine and book pairings and exhibitions. Whether you're there for an event, to work or to browse the stacks, the Center is guaranteed to inspire.

54   LEFT BANK BOOKS

399 North Euclid Avenue, St. Louis, MO 63108, USA

While it may not be as famous as the Gateway Arch, Left Bank Books is just as much a St. Louis landmark. The independent bookstore was founded in 1969 by a group of Washington University grad students and for over 50 years it has not only been a place to buy new and used books but also a cultural institution. It hosts over 300 events each year, showcasing the talents of famous authors and local poets, and offers eight book clubs and pop-up reading groups. Left Bank prides itself on giving back to the local community and has several initiatives to promote literacy amongst St. Louisans.

55 ELLIOTT BAY BOOK COMPANY

1521 10th Avenue, Seattle, WA 98122, USA

TO VISIT
BEFORE YOU DIE
BECAUSE

You can spend hours browsing the thousands of books in this beloved Seattle store.

Elliott Bay Book Company has been a Seattle institution since it opened in its original Pioneer Square location in 1973. In 2010, the independent bookstore moved to the Capitol Hill neighborhood, where it occupies a bright, expansive multi-level space filled with over 150,000 books. Elliott Bay hosts multiple in-person and virtual author events weekly and has monthly book groups on themes including global issues and sci-fi and fantasy. The knowledgeable booksellers can provide recommendations, or you can sign up for one of their monthly subscriptions of first editions, poetry, romance, true crime or graphic novels. Its Little Oddfellows café is the ideal spot to flip through your purchases over a coffee and a pastry.

56 THE DRAMA BOOK SHOP

266 West 39th Street, New York, NY 10018, USA

TO VISIT
BEFORE YOU DIE
BECAUSE

This Tony
Award-winning
bookstore is one
of the world's
best resources
for lovers of the
stage.

The Drama Book Shop has been a fixture of the New York theater scene since it was founded in 1917. When it nearly closed in 2019, the creator of the musical *Hamilton*, Lin-Manuel Miranda, together with the show's director, producer and theater owner, stepped in to save the beloved, quirky store, which reopened in a wondrous new space on West 39th Street in 2021. *Hamilton* scenic designer David Korins set the stage, taking inspiration from 20th-century European reading rooms and cafés. A "bookworm" spirals through the shop, where you can find plays and musicals, books on acting, writing, costume design, and theater history and criticism.

57   LIBRERÍA MÁS PURO VERSO

Peatonal Sarandí 675, 11000 Montevideo, Uruguay

TO VISIT
BEFORE YOU DIE
BECAUSE

The store's
Art Nouveau
setting is truly
transporting.

Located in the Ciudad Vieja area of Montevideo, Librería Más Puro Verso is a must-visit for book and architecture fans. The bookstore is housed in the Pablo Ferrando Building, a spectacular Art Nouveau structure built by architect Leopoldo Tosi in 1917. The centerpiece of the store is the stained glass window and clock above the marble staircase, and period details abound throughout the store, including elegant iron and plaster work. The store features a café and restaurant should you work up an appetite browsing the impressive selection of books and music.

58   RIZOMA

Calle Los Lobos between Calle José Ignacio and
Calle República Argentina, La Juanita, Maldonado, Uruguay

TO VISIT
BEFORE YOU DIE
BECAUSE

This gorgeous
bookstore–hotel
hybrid should
be on every
bibliophile's
bucket list.

Rizoma is the kind of bookstore that beckons you to stay awhile. Overnight, in fact. The business in La Juanita on the southern coast of Uruguay combines a bookstore, hotel, art gallery and restaurant all in one exquisitely designed complex. The store carries over 15,000 titles, including works on philosophy, photography, cooking and poetry, all arranged in a series of incredible wood-lined, soaring spaces. Owner Eduardo Ballester opened Rizoma in late 2020, and the project is a family affair—guests can find ceramics by his wife, Marcela Jacob, in the gallery.

59 YANJIYOU CAPSULE BOOKSTORE

East side of Liuyun Xiangshu Hotel, Tonglu County, Zhejiang Province, China

TO VISIT
BEFORE YOU DIE
BECAUSE

It's an architectural wonder set in an awe-inspiring natural landscape.

Nested in the forest of Tonglu in Zhejiang Province, Yanjiyou Capsule Bookstore is worth the trip for book and nature lovers alike. Architecture firm Atelier tao + c repurposed an old two-story wood and mud building on the rural site, adding a capsule hotel with 20 sleeping spaces, a bookstore and a library. Shelves made of local bamboo line the double-height space, and visitors can enjoy a book and the view of the surrounding landscape in the sunken reading room or the curved sitting area beside the towering transparent eastern façade.

60   COMMON READER

1F, Guigu International Center, No. 2000 Shixinbei Road,
Xiaoshan District, Hangzhou City, Zhejiang Province, China

Inspired by the Virginia Woolf book of the same name, Common Reader was created to be more than just a retail space; it was designed as a place to learn and enjoy the reading experience. Architecture firm Atelier tao + c devised an intimate space with green velvet curtains, bookshelves and seats made of dark cherry wood, and green reading lights that nod to the feel of old libraries. Reading nooks are set up throughout the store and are specifically designed to encourage visitors to sit down and stay awhile.

61 SHSH BY JETLAG BOOKS

303-2, Dongsi North Street, Dongcheng District, Beijing, China

TO VISIT
BEFORE YOU DIE
BECAUSE

Jetlag Books offers creative books and magazines in a gallery-like setting.

Founded in 2020, Beijing's hip Jetlag Books reinvents the city news-stand by offering a carefully selected array of magazines and books in inventive settings. Its latest outpost, SHSH by Jetlag Books, opened in 2022 alongside the Chinese co-working space company 5lmeet, and is part bookstore, part café and part co-working space. The contemporary interior was transformed by +C Architects, who added inventive rotating stainless-steel shelves that provide a sleek contrast to the rough concrete walls and acrylic displays that make the books on art, design, fashion and poetry appear to float. Once you find your source of inspiration du jour, you can grab a seat at the bar along the window-lined storefront and watch the world go by.

62   ZHAOXI BOOKSTORE

2F, Longhuli, No. 67-3, South Longhu Zhonghuan Road Jiuru Road, Jinshui District, Zhengzhou City, Henan Province, China

TO VISIT
BEFORE YOU DIE
BECAUSE

The peaceful bookstore is a welcome respite from the hustle and bustle of the city.

Architecture firm Atelier tao + c designed Zhaoxi Bookstore to be a calm destination in a busy shopping center in the Zhengdong New District of Zhengzhou. The store serves as a gathering place for neighborhood residents and includes a bar, café, auditorium and reading areas for both adults and children. Arched and rectangular passageways lead shoppers between the different sections of the store and create a sense of modern grandeur, while the white walls and minimalist shelving make it easy to browse and allow the books to be center stage.

No Website   +86 17335569090

63   **READING MI**

L3 Floor, Shuncheng Darong City, No. 30 Nanguo East Road, Jinliang Community, Daliang Street, Shunde District, Foshan City, China

This architectural stunner of a bookstore feels like a cathedral of knowledge.

It's easy to forget that Reading Mi is located in the central atrium of a busy shopping center in Foshan. The serene bookstore was designed by Panorama Design Group to be a place of exploration and cultural conversation. Visitors enter through the awe-inspiring "Hall of Knowledge," a double-height space topped with wooden slats that recall the shape of an open book. The nearly 27,000-square foot store is filled with peaceful areas to read, a 100-seat theater, a café and a delightful family zone outfitted with thousands of children's books and a stage for storytelling.

64   PAGE ONE

28 Chengfu Road, Wudaokou, Haidian District,
Beijing, China

With floor-to-ceiling books, you can immerse yourself in the store's maze-like atmosphere.

Set on a busy concourse, PAGE ONE's location in the Haidian District of Beijing was designed to be an integral part of the neighborhood and caters to shoppers looking to linger as well as passersby on their daily commutes. The design studio Office AIO planned the interior of the store to be immersive. Visitors can climb the book-lined staircase to the second floor and browse through the maze of bookcases. Once you find your next read, enjoy a cup of coffee in the café and watch the world go by on the bustling plaza outside, or grab a drink from the to-go counter and browse the displays of open books set up for window reading.

65 YAN

The MixC, Luohu District, Shenzhen,
Guangdong Province, China

The store's
Zen-Buddhism–
inspired design
makes it a
peaceful place
to find your next
read.

Set on the third floor of the MixC commercial complex in Shenzen,
Yan is a warm and sophisticated shopping experience. Architect
Tomoko Ikegai of ikg inc. wanted the over 26,000-square-foot
store to be a place of self-discovery and cultural exchange. Visitors
are welcomed by striking rammed earth walls, and natural hues
and materials create a calming environment throughout the Zen-
Buddhism–inspired space. Curl up with a new title on the plush pur-
ple velvet sofas after browsing the golden shelves. The store includes
event, gathering and café spaces, and five original artworks have
been installed in the space.

66   TENGDA ZHONGSHUGE

3F Tengda Center Building, Taizhou City,
Zhejiang Province, China

TO VISIT
BEFORE YOU DIE
BECAUSE

A trip to the landscape-inspired store feels like you're browsing in a surrealist work of art.

Zhongshuge is known for its maximalist bookstores, and its Taizhou City branch is no exception. The surrealist store was designed by ETER Architecture Design, which drew inspiration for the store's interiors from the local landscape, including Tiantai Mountain and the Haishan Islands. Circular displays float beneath the rippling ceiling, which recalls the surface of water, while in another space, bookcases climb towards the mirrors above. The children's area is a colorful wonderland with design elements influenced by local folk customs. Velvet-covered seating areas offer plush spots to enjoy a coffee from the café and take in the splendid surroundings.

67 CHAMPACA BOOKSTORE

7/1 Edward Road, Off Queens Road, Bengaluru-560051, India

TO VISIT
BEFORE YOU DIE
BECAUSE

You'll find books by a diverse selection of authors in a tree house–like space.

Named after the flowering tree, Champaca Bookstore is a woman-owned independent bookstore in Bengaluru that opened in 2019. Visiting the lush roof-top store feels like shopping in a tree house, and it's the perfect retreat from the hustle and bustle of the city. Champaca is a community space dedicated to showcasing a diverse selection of voices. It hosts engaging virtual and in-person discussions and workshops and encourages literacy with its reading challenges for adults and a children's library for younger browsers. The store also offers book club subscriptions focused on a yearly topic such as translation, travel or loneliness and connection. In 2022, Champaca opened a new branch in Goa.

champaca.in   +91-93536-08989

68 POST

Lantai Atas, Blok B 22-23 & 66-67, Jl. Cipaku No. 1, Kebayoran Baru, Jakarta Selatan, Indonesia

TO VISIT
BEFORE YOU DIE
BECAUSE

This small shop is full of unique, hard-to-find books, many from independent publishers.

Located on the upper level of Pasar Santa, a traditional market in Jakarta Selatan, POST is a fiercely independent bookstore. All the volumes in the compact shop are chosen by the booksellers and include under-the-radar titles that you won't find in bigger bookstores, including books from Indonesian publishers. The shop hosts writing workshops as well as book launches and discussion groups. Since 2016, owners Maesy Ang and Teddy Wijaya Kusuma have also operated a publishing arm known as POST Press, putting out a small but mighty selection of books it absolutely loves.

69   SIPUR PASHUT

Shabazi Street 36, Neve Tzedek, Tel Aviv-Yafo 6515038, Israel

The colorful Tel Aviv-Yafo store is nurturing the next generation of writers.

Founded in 2003, Sipur Pashut, which translates as "a simple story," is an independent bookstore set in the Neve Tzedek neighborhood of Tel Aviv-Yafo. The colorful two-story store, which is accentuated with vibrantly painted ironwork, was named after the book by Shai Agnon, the legendary Israeli novelist and Nobel laureate who lived and worked in the area. In addition to offering an extensive selection of books in Hebrew and English, including significant poetry and Israeli graphic novel sections, the store serves as a showcase for writers and illustrators with writing workshops, readings, book launches and cultural events.

70 THE BOOKSHOP AT THE AMERICAN COLONY HOTEL

1 Louis Vincent Street, East Jerusalem, Israel

TO VISIT
BEFORE YOU DIE
BECAUSE

The Bookshop has a wealth of texts about the region's politics, culture and religions.

You can find a treasure trove of knowledge at The Bookshop at the American Colony Hotel in Jerusalem. Owned and operated by Palestinian cultural leader Mahmoud Muna, also known as The Bookseller of Jerusalem, the small but impressive shop is located in the historic hotel and offers a comprehensive selection of English-language volumes on the history, politics, culture and religions of the region as well as contemporary fiction. The shop has counted an array of literary figures as visitors and customers over the years, so take a cue from them and find a fascinating read, then enjoy it on the hotel's lovely terrace just outside the shop.

71 TEHRAN BOOK GARDEN

Taran Western Side of the National Library Boulevard,
Haghani Highway, Tehran 11369, Iran

TO VISIT
BEFORE YOU DIE
BECAUSE

The largest
bookstore in
Iran has 700,000
square feet to
explore.

With the largest collection of books in Iran, Tehran Book Garden, or Baghe Ketab, is a wonderland for adult and child readers. The nearly 700,000-square-foot complex has three floors of attractions for all ages and is divided into four blocks. The building is topped with a sprawling roof garden, which is home to cafés and a summer cinema. Visitors can shop in the adult and kid's bookstores and then explore the movie theaters, art gallery, escape room, two science parks for kids, art shop, prayer room, restaurants and exhibition spaces.

72 DAIKANYAMA T-SITE

17-5 Sarugakucho, Shibuya-ku, Tokyo 150-0033, Japan

TO VISIT
BEFORE YOU DIE
BECAUSE

With a restaurant, co-working space and cocktail lounge, you can spend all day at Daikanyama T-Site.

Often called one of the most beautiful bookstores in the world, Daikanyama T-Site is an entire campus of culture. The complex is made up of three buildings, clad in the iconic T-latticed façade and connected by a passage known as Magazine Street. The bookstore is stocked with Japanese and English books, and the stationery store has an array of papers and writing utensils. Concierges are on hand to help you find just the right purchase. At the Anjin Library & Lounge, magazine fans can browse 30,000 vintage issues, including many from the 60s and 70s. If you're looking to get some work done, the recently added Share Lounge co-working space is just the spot.

store.tsite.jp/daikanyama/english   03-3770-2525

73   NANYODO

1-21 Kanda Jimbocho, Chiyoda-ku Tokyo 101-0051, Japan

TO VISIT
BEFORE YOU DIE
BECAUSE

Nanyodo is a
wonderland for
architecture and
design buffs.

Architecture fans are sure to find something that's right up their alley at Nanyodo, an independent bookstore in Tokyo. The store was established in the 1920s and focuses on titles related to architecture, design and urbanism. Explore the eye-catching concrete block–clad store's three floors of Japanese and international books, magazines and rare volumes. Find titles on architects and designers from Aalto to Zumthor, as well as technical guides and criticism. The store is also known for its occasional Window Gallery displays, where architects sketch on the store's large glass front window.

74   NOSTOS

5-1-18-102 Kinuta, Setagaya-ku, Tokyo 157-0073, Japan

TO VISIT
BEFORE YOU DIE
BECAUSE

You can find your new favorite book as well as a chic selection of gifts.

Browse a beautifully curated selection of books and other treasures in an equally chic space at Nostos, a petite bookstore in the trendy Setagaya neighborhood of Tokyo. The store, which began as an online shop in 2012 and moved to its current location in 2021, specializes in secondhand volumes on art, design, crafts and photography. Discover pre-loved books on everything from typography and gardening to textile design and cooking displayed alongside stylish gifts such as incense, leather goods, pottery, cashmere accessories and artful calendars. The store is currently open on Wednesday, Saturday and Sunday afternoons.

75   BUNKITSU

Roppongi Electric Building 1F, 6-1-20 Roppongi, Minato-ku, Tokyo 106-0032, Japan

TO VISIT
BEFORE YOU DIE
BECAUSE

This beautifully designed store is worth the price of admission.

Bunkitsu is an innovative concept bookstore in Roppongi that offers peaceful browsing for a small price. Admission is 1,650 yen (around $11) on weekdays and 2,530 yen (about $17) on weekends and holidays. Once inside, you can enjoy coffee or green tea and 30,000 books that include art, design, literature and food titles. The store has plenty of spaces to work or sit and examine the books and magazines on offer. Visitors will also find special exhibitions and 90 magazines next to the entrance on the first floor and a café with food and drinks on the second level.

76   BOOKS@CAFE

Omar Bin Al-Khattab Street 12, Amman, Jordan

TO VISIT
BEFORE YOU DIE
BECAUSE

The cheery patterns and delicious dishes are sure to put a smile on your face.

Books@Cafe's story began in 1997 when it opened in Jabal Amman as the Middle East's first internet café. Today, it is a lively bookstore and community hub complete with a restaurant, bar, gift shop and art gallery. The interior is decorated with eye-popping prints, including graphic black and white stripes and Marimekko-style florals, and you'll find a large selection of books in English and Arabic in its colorful rooms. Once you've finished browsing, enjoy a meal or a cocktail on one of the beautiful terraces. Books@Cafe is open until midnight for late-night book needs.

77 GERAKBUDAYA BOOKSHOP

226 Lebuh Pantai, George Town, 10300 Penang, Malaysia

TO VISIT
BEFORE YOU DIE
BECAUSE

The cheery shop is a literary hub in a UNESCO World Heritage Site.

Founded by writer and editor Gareth Richards in 2014, Gerakbudaya Bookshop is a cultural hub in the UNESCO World Heritage site of George Town. Located in the Hikayat complex, the sunny yellow shop is dedicated to encouraging literacy and critical thinking in Penang, whether through its pop-up book stalls at community centers and festivals or its program of book launches and author discussions. Each of the enthusiastic staff members curates a section of the shop, and shoppers will find over 6,000 titles covering everything from Southeast Asian studies to literary fiction and the environment.

78 SORISOMOON BOOKS

8-31, Jeojidong-gil, Hangyeong-myeon, Jeju-si,
Jeju-do 63005, Republic of Korea

TO VISIT
BEFORE YOU DIE
BECAUSE

The Jeju Island store has a carefully selected list of books in a beautiful remote space.

Sorisomoon is as much an experience as it is a bookstore. No detail was too small for the booksellers as they created a highly curated environment for browsing and reading. The wood-lined interior of the main display areas creates a rustic cabin feel, and the store is filled with spaces to explore and carefully chosen books to browse. You'll find places to work, as well as spots where you can rest and enjoy a book. If you're feeling adventurous, take a chance with one of the wrapped "blind books."

79 SEOUL CHAEKBOGO

1, Ogeum-ro, Songpa-gu, Seoul, Republic of Korea

TO VISIT BEFORE YOU DIE BECAUSE

You can get lost for hours in the tunnel of secondhand books.

Many of Seoul's used bookstores came together to create Seoul CHAEKBOGO, a spectacular secondhand bookstore with a mission to show customers the value of old books. The volumes are organized according to the bookstore they came from, and a computer system will help you if you're on the hunt for a specific title. Steel arch bookcases create a striking tunnel in which to browse (and take a few pictures for Instagram). The store is also home to a café, an area with independent publications, and exhibition and event spaces, where visitors can explore books donated by noteworthy figures, view temporary exhibits and experience lectures and other cultural programs.

80 ESLITE SPECTRUM TAICHUNG CHUNGYO STORE

10F, No. 161, Section 3, Sanmin Road, North District,
Taichung City 404, Taiwan

TO VISIT
BEFORE YOU DIE
BECAUSE

The ring of
bookcases
makes you feel
surrounded by
texts.

Eslite has been selling books in Taiwan since it opened its first store in 1989, and today it operates over 40 stores in Taiwan, Hong Kong, China and Japan. One of its most impressive outposts is the Eslite Spectrum Taichung Chungyo Store in the central region of the country. The store's design concept was a bookstore that "crosses time and space," and noted architect Ray Chen did just that by filling the 26-foot high interior with an eye-catching ring of bookcases. Explore the multiple curved levels, then find a seat on the rows of benches on the lowest level where you will be surrounded by a sea of books.

81 THE BOOKSMITH

The Booksmith@Nimman 1/1-1/5 Nimmanhaemin Road, Suthep, Mueang Chiang Mai District, Chiang Mai 50200, Thailand

TO VISIT
BEFORE YOU DIE
BECAUSE

The Chiang
Mai bookstore
specializes in art
and design titles.

The Booksmith has been an independent purveyor of books in Chiang Mai since Sirote Jiraprayoon founded the company in 2012. You'll find a wide variety of titles at the flagship store set within the One Nimman complex, although its catalog really shines in its art and design section. Shoppers can discover hard-to-find books and magazines in the lovely space, which features exposed brick walls and charming tile floors. Grab a drink at the café, known as Chillax Corner, and dive into a gorgeous monograph or an international design magazine. Booksmith also has branches at the Donmuang and Chiang Mai airports should you need a last-minute plane read.

82 OPEN HOUSE BOOKSHOP BY HARDCOVER

1030 Phloen Chit Road, Lumphini, Pathum Wan, Bangkok 10330, Thailand

TO VISIT
BEFORE YOU DIE
BECAUSE

You'll find an exceptional selection of new and hard-to-find art books in a bright, airy space.

Set within the bustling Central Embassy shopping complex, Open House Bookshop by Hardcover is a spacious and airy purveyor of new and hard-to-find books. Shoppers will find a comprehensive lineup of books with a particular focus on art, design and culture at the outpost, which is operated by Hardcover: The Art Book Shop. Browse volumes on everything from ceramics to textiles and travel, as well as sections on the arts and culture of Thailand, Korea, China, Japan, Islam, India and the Himalayas. Then enjoy your finds in the light-filled seating areas, bars and restaurants.

83 LIBRAIRIE TROPISMES

11, Galerie des Princes, Galeries Royale Saint-Hubert,
B-1000 Brussels, Belgium

Its magnificent setting in a mid-19th-century Brussels gallery is a must-see.

Browse an array of French-language titles in a stunning space at Librairie Tropismes. Founded in 1984, the bookstore is located in the Galeries Royale Saint-Hubert, a spectacular 1847 structure by architect Jean-Pierre Cluysenaar. The store has expanded multiple times over the years and now spans three levels. You'll feel like you're at a 19th-century ball as you peruse literature, fine arts volumes and children's books beneath the soaring ornate ceilings and columns. Head up to the mezzanine for the best views of the store, with its mirrored walls, gilded columns and endless stacks of books.

84   COOK & BOOK

Place du Temps Libre 1,
1200 Woluwe-Saint-Lambert, Belgium

TO VISIT
BEFORE YOU DIE
BECAUSE

**Cook & Book
is a literary
and culinary
experience that's
not to be missed.**

Many bookstores have cafés where you can grab a coffee and a pastry, but Cook & Book takes bookstore dining to the next level. The store is spread over two buildings (Bloc A and Bloc B) filled with nine creatively designed sections, from the travel section, complete with an Airstream trailer, to the colorful neon-lit fine arts section. 800 books are suspended over the literature room, and the cooking section is modeled after an Italian trattoria. Dining areas are spread throughout the sections.

85 LUDDITES BOOKS & WINE

Hopland 34, 2000 Antwerp, Belgium

TO VISIT
BEFORE YOU DIE
BECAUSE

This chic Antwerp store proves that nothing pairs better with wine than a good book.

Luddites Books & Wine is a bookstore, wine bar and safe haven for those who want to escape the digital world. The store, which opened in 2020, is located in the center of Antwerp in a 1902 neoclassical townhouse designed by architect Jules Bilmeyer. Luddites offers the largest selection of English books in the city as well as plenty of Dutch titles in its beautifully designed spaces, which feature rolling library ladders and books tucked into fireplaces. Climb the stairs to visit the wine bar, where you can enjoy a carefully chosen selection of wines by the glass or bottle, as well as coffee, tea and snacks.

luddites.be

03 298 55 33

86 BOEKENHUIS THEORIA

Casinoplein 10, 8500 Kortrijk, Belgium

TO VISIT
BEFORE YOU DIE
BECAUSE

This storied
neoclassical
building's latest
incarnation—a
bookstore—is its
best yet.

The gorgeous neoclassical building in Kortrijk has had many lives. Over the years, it has been a bank, a school, a concert hall and a casino, but its latest and perhaps best incarnation is as Boekenhuis Theoria, a grand independent bookstore with a selection of books that lives up to its beautiful setting. Architectural details—from Ionic columns to black-and-white marble floors and a stately staircase—abound, and the store is home to a soaring event space and a charming café where shoppers can take a break with a coffee and a piece of cake.

87 FRAKTURA

Kneza Mislava 17, 10 000 Zagreb, Croatia

Family-owned Croatian publishing company Fraktura opened its brick-and-mortar bookstore in Zagreb in 2020. The store stocks the company's award-winning books alongside releases from other publishers, including fiction, non-fiction, monographs and comics, in a location they call "a living room for all book lovers." The dramatic black-walled space features soaring shelves piled high with books, and browsers should be sure to look up: the ceiling was painted by Tomislav Buntak, a painter and dean of the Academy of Fine Arts, who painted each of the surface's niches with characters from classic literature.

fraktura.hr 01/581-4624

88   RÜSTEM KITABEVI

Girne Caddesi No. 26 Lefkosa, Nicosia, Cyprus

The marvelous Rüstem Kitabevi is a cultural center of Cyprus.

Since its opening in 1937, Rüstem Kitabevi has been a beloved meeting space and cultural hub for the residents of Nicosia. The family-owned business began as a purveyor of novels, maps and travel guides, and over the years it has expanded more than just its stock, which now includes an assortment of books in English, Turkish and German. Rüstem became a publisher in the 1950s and has added a café, restaurant and gallery. Browse through the eclectic interiors, then sit beneath the trees in the shady courtyard, where the store hosts frequent events, including performance art, antique markets and jazz concerts.

     rustembookshop.wordpress.com   +90 392 228 35 06

89 BOOKS & COMPANY

Sofievej 1, 2900 Hellerup, Denmark

TO VISIT
BEFORE YOU DIE
BECAUSE

The charming store near Copenhagen places a strong emphasis on community.

Books & Company in the suburbs of Copenhagen puts a special emphasis on the second part of its name. The store, which opened in 2009, prides itself on being a community hub where customers can meet up to chat, sit and read, or browse the well-curated selection of books, international magazines and newspapers. Grab a coffee and find a cozy spot in the warm and welcoming store, which also hosts ten book clubs, each with a different theme, including fiction, non-fiction, social issues, human sexuality, translated fiction and personal empowerment.

booksandcompany.dk +45 39 30 40 45

90 NEW MAGS

Ny Østergade 28, 1101 Copenhagen, Denmark

The gallery-like setting is the perfect spot to browse the artsy books and magazines.

New Mags prides itself on selling the coolest and most stylish reading material in the world. The distributor's Copenhagen bookstore, designed by Norm Architects, is a fitting setting for their immaculately curated selection of books, magazines and objects. Warm wood lines the walls of the minimalist store, which feels part library, part art gallery. Stone plinths, an oak study table, wood shelves and a sleek steel table display the covers of books and magazines like works of art. Design, art and photography fans will find an array of lifestyle books they'll want to add to their collections and coffee tables.

new-mags.com +45 536 19 169

91   GAY'S THE WORD

66 Marchmont Street, London WC1N 1AB, England

Founded in 1979, Gay's The Word is the UK's oldest LGBTQIA+ bookstore and a vital community hub. Over the years, the store has been the meeting spot for many LGBT groups, including the Lesbian Discussion Group, which has been meeting there for over 40 years, and Lesbians and Gays Support the Miners in the 1980s. The pioneering store is packed with books in a variety of genres, from biographies to LGBT history, as well as a selection of rare and used titles. Gay's The Word also stays true to its socialist roots and all profits are reinvested into the store.

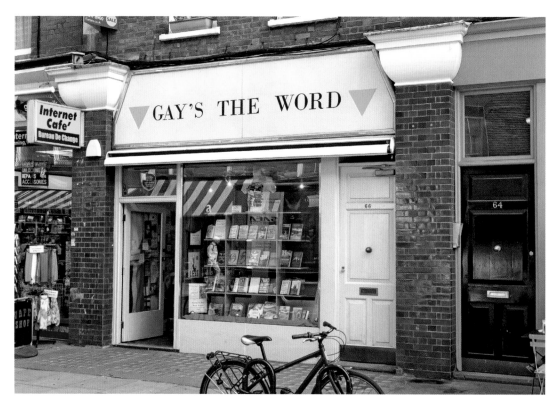

92   BARTER BOOKS

Alnwick Station, Northumberland NE66 2NP, England

TO VISIT
BEFORE YOU DIE
BECAUSE

The *New Statesman* described Barter Books as the "British Library of secondhand bookshops."

In 1991, Mary and Stuart Manley opened Barter Books, their beloved secondhand bookstore set in a Victorian train station in Northumberland. This truly one-of-a-kind bookstore offers an incredible selection in a remarkable setting, including the soaring main hall, which was once part of the outgoing platform. The store is complete with Paradise, an ice cream parlor, and the Station Buffet, a café with tables set up in the former first-class sitting areas. In the winter, shoppers can curl up by the functioning fireplace in the beautiful old waiting room. If you find yourself short of funds, you can barter your old titles for new (at least new to you) secondhand volumes.

93　HEYWOOD HILL

10 Curzon Street, London W1J 5HH, England

TO VISIT
BEFORE YOU DIE
BECAUSE

The former
workplace of
Nancy Mitford
offers a delightful
shopping
experience.

Heywood Hill opened his iconic bookstore on Curzon Street in 1936, and over the years it has become a beloved London institution known for its superior service and mix of books, catering to everyone from kids to collectors. Set in a Georgian townhouse, Heywood Hill offers new, old and antiquarian books in a sophisticated but inviting locale. Novelist Nancy Mitford worked in the store during World War II and is credited with establishing the enjoyable tone that remains to this day. The bookseller offers subscriptions of 12–40 books a year and will even design a custom-made library of books for shoppers with empty shelves.

　　　　heywoodhill.com　　　　+44 20 7629 0647

94   HATCHARD'S

187 Piccadilly, London, W1J 9LE, England

The oldest bookstore in London is beloved by readers and royals.

Located on bustling Piccadilly, Hatchard's is London's oldest bookstore. Publisher and anti-slavery campaigner John Hatchard founded the store in 1797, and for over 225 years it has been a beloved literary landmark in the city. The five-story Georgian store has long been the bookseller of choice for the Royal Family, dating back to Queen Charlotte, wife of King George III, who was one of Hatchard's first customers. Climb the central staircase to explore floor after floor, and don't miss the robust crime and mystery section and the beautifully designed editions of classics by P.G. Wodehouse, Daphne du Maurier and more.

hatchards.co.uk   020 7439 9921

95 BLACKWELL'S

48-51 Broad Street, Oxford OX1 3BQ, England

TO VISIT
BEFORE YOU DIE
BECAUSE

Blackwell's went from humble beginnings in a 12-square-foot room to a record-setting space.

Benjamin Blackwell opened his first bookstore in a 12-square-foot room at 50 Broad Street in Oxford in 1879. Since then, the company has expanded to include over 20 stores, and the original location has also grown—including underground. The store is now spread across four storefronts, and in the 60s, Blackwell's developed the Norrington Room, a cavernous basement chamber created by tunneling under a section of Trinity College. *The Guinness Book of World Records* once listed the Norrington Room as the single largest room in the world selling books. The company was run by the Blackwell family for over 140 years until Waterstones purchased it in 2022.

blackwells.co.uk
01865 792792

96 PERSEPHONE BOOKS

8 Edgar Buildings, Bath BA1 2EE, England

Persephone Books began in 1998 as a small publishing imprint dedicated to re-publishing out-of-print or overlooked works by female writers of the 20th century. Founder Nicola Beauman later expanded her enterprise to include a bookstore, which from 2021 has been located in a 1761 building in Bath. Shoppers can find all of the company's beautifully designed dove-gray releases (now numbering over 145), including their biggest hit, *Miss Pettigrew Lives for a Day*, in the elegant space. Should you fall in love with their titles and want to build your own library, the company offers a book-a-month subscription, and local readers can attend events or join a monthly book group.

persephonebooks.co.uk 01225 425050

97   WORD ON THE WATER

Regent's Canal Towpath, London N1C 4LW, England

TO VISIT
BEFORE YOU DIE
BECAUSE

You can find your next read at this unique floating bookstore in London.

Housed in a 1920s Dutch barge, Word on the Water is a floating bookstore in London's Regent's Canal Towpath. The one-of-a-kind store offers everything from classics and contemporary fiction to art and photography titles, as well as some unexpected finds in the cozy space, which is warmed by a wood-burning stove in the winter months. The wood-paneled interior overflows with books, which also line the towpath side of the exterior, and the children's section is a treat for young readers. Word on the Water also hosts poetry readings and jazz concerts on the barge's roof.

98   DAUNT BOOKS

84 Marylebone High Street, London W1U 4QW, England

The three-level travel section set in an Edwardian-era space feels like a trip back in time.

Stepping into Daunt Books' Marylebone location feels like stepping back in time. Head into the travel section of the Edwardian bookstore to explore the three-level space with its oak balconies, stained glass window and soaring skylights. Globetrotters will find guides, history books, language references and other topics arranged by country, with the British Isles in the upper gallery, Europe on the main level, and the rest of the world tucked downstairs. The rest of the store contains an excellent selection of fiction and non-fiction, but it's the travel section that makes Daunt a must-visit.

dauntbooks.co.uk   020 7224 2295

99 LIBRAIRIE JOUSSEAUME

45-46-47 Galerie Vivienne, 75002 Paris, France

TO VISIT
BEFORE YOU DIE
BECAUSE

The beautiful bookstore is located in one of Paris's dreamy covered passages.

Stroll through Galerie Vivienne, one of Paris's elegant covered passages, to find Librairie Jousseaume. The passageway opened in 1826, with a bookstore as one of its original tenants. In 1890, the store was acquired and became Librairie Jousseaume. Today the store, which is split into two stores across from each other, is run by the owner's great-grandson François Jousseaume, who stocks a wide variety of antique, used and modern books from the 19th and 20th centuries, as well as prints and engravings. The two stores feature wondrous details such as a wooden spiral staircase, glowing chandeliers and towering shelves, creating a beautiful spot to browse.

100 BOUQUINISTES

The Seine, Paris, France

There's nothing like picking up a beautiful book while strolling along the Seine.

Head to the Seine to browse the offering of Paris's famous bouquinistes who peddle their wares from 900 green boxes along both banks of the river. The charming stands have been around since the 16th century, and novelist Honoré de Balzac once described them as "catacombs of glory." Find used and rare books, as well as prints and posters at the hundreds of open-air stores, which stretch from Pont Marie to Quai du Louvre on the Right Bank and from Quai de la Tournelle to Quai Voltaire on the Left Bank. The bouquinistes, along with the banks of the Seine, were named a UNESCO World Heritage site in 1991.

No Website   No Telephone Number

101 SHAKESPEARE AND COMPANY

37 rue de la Bûcherie, 75005 Paris, France

It is one of the most famous bookstores in the world.

The gold standard of independent bookstores, Shakespeare and Company has been attracting crowds of eager readers since George Whitman founded the store in 1951 as Le Mistral. It was renamed Shakespeare and Company in 1964 in honor of bookseller Sylvia Beach's influential store of the same name—a favorite of early 20th-century ex-pat writers. Located on Paris's Left Bank in an early 17th-century building that was originally a monastery, the literary institution offers new, second-hand and antiquarian books in a history-filled setting. The store also houses aspiring writers, known as "tumbleweeds," who sleep in beds tucked within the shelves in exchange for helping in the store. Today Whitman's daughter, Sylvia, is at the helm, and the store now has a café, a literary prize, a publishing arm and a podcast.

shakespeareandcompany.com   +33 1 43 25 40 93

EUROPE FRANCE

102 LIBRAIRIE ACTES SUD

Place Nina Berberova, 13200 Arles, France

TO VISIT
BEFORE YOU DIE
BECAUSE

The store is
more than just a
bookstore; it's a
cultural complex.

There's something for everyone at Librairie Actes Sud in Arles. The store, founded in 1983, is part of Passage du Méjan, a complex containing the bookstore, a cinema, a restaurant, a theater, an exhibition space and a hammam all in one place. Find books published by Actes Sud, as well as 40,000 other titles and a large selection of classical, jazz and world music in the over 3,000-square-foot space. Browse the store, then take in a movie at Cinémas Actes Sud or relax at Hammam Chiffa.

librairieactessud.com 04 90 49 56 77

103 VIEILLE BOURSE BOOK MARKET

Place du Général de Gaulle, 59000 Lille, France

You'll find all sorts of treasures in the courtyard of this architectural wonder.

No trip to Lille would be complete without a visit to the Vieille Bourse Book Market. The market is set in the courtyard of the monumental former stock exchange, which was constructed in 1653 by Julien Destrée in the Flemish Renaissance style. Tables of second-hand books line the space, and you'll find everything from leather-bound French classics to comic books, as well as posters, vintage newspapers and other ephemera. The market operates in the afternoons, Tuesday through Sunday, and in the summer you can stick around to see the tango demonstrations on Sunday evenings.

104 BÜCHERBOGEN AM SAVIGNYPLATZ

Savignyplatz, Stadtbahnbogen 593, 10623 Berlin, Germany

TO VISIT
BEFORE YOU DIE
BECAUSE

The store's unique setting and its collection of art, fashion, film and design books make it a must-see.

Founded in 1980, Bücherbogen am Savignyplatz is an epic bookstore set in a brick viaduct under the railway tracks in the Charlottenburg area of Berlin. Owner Ruthild Spangenberg started out with two archways, and over the years the store has expanded to fill five. Bücherbogen's vaulted rooms focus on art, film, fashion and design, so it's no wonder the store was a favorite of fashion designer Karl Lagerfeld. In addition to the thousands of volumes on offer, including magazines, exhibition catalogs and books on theory, art lovers can also find rare volumes in the antiquarian section.

105   ANTIQUARIAT ALT-HOHENECK

Untere Gasse 29, 71642 Ludwigsburg, Germany

**TO VISIT
BEFORE YOU DIE
BECAUSE**

You can browse this antiquarian bookstore 24/7.

If you've ever needed a new book at an odd hour of the day or night, then Antiquariat Alt-Hoheneck is the store of your dreams. The outdoor antiquarian bookstore is open 24 hours a day, seven days a week, and offers around 7,000 books, which shoppers can buy by putting the price on the front of the book in the register. More precious volumes are sold at the indoor store across the street, which stocks 9,000 titles and 3,000 records, and an upper level houses 15,000 books. Antiquariat Alt-Hoheneck also hosts a summer bookshop the second weekend of each month from April to September with 40,000 titles, and an annual book market each September.

           antiquariat-althoheneck.de   +49 7141 649639

106 PRO QM

Almstadtstrasse 48-50, D-10119 Berlin, Germany

Founded in 1999 by Katja Reichard, Axel J. Wieder and Jesko Fezer, Pro qm is a specialized bookstore focused on the city and its connections to politics, the economy, pop culture, architecture, design and art theory. The highly focused store is set in a 1920s building in the Berlin-Mitte District designed by modern architect Hans Poelzig with a bright, contemporary interior outfitted by ifau und Jesko Fezer. The international and German books and magazines are often arranged thematically around emerging issues, and customers will discover a tightly curated assortment of books on urbanism, art, music and more.

107 OCELOT

Brunnenstrasse 181, 10119 Berlin, Germany

Ocelot's tagline is "not just another bookstore," and the Berlin store endeavors to be more than just a place to buy the latest bestseller. The staff aim to match customers with the right book, and once that match is made, the welcoming space invites shoppers to stay awhile. The modern interior by Martina Zeyen mixes industrial elements with warm wood walls and bookcases, creating a stylish setting for the store's events, which include discussion groups, book signings and launches. Kids will find a large section of children's books toward the rear of the store, while adults can browse the hand-picked novels, cookbooks and more throughout the rest of the space.

genialokal.de/buchhandlung/berlin/ocelot   030 97894592

108   ZABRISKIE

Reichenberger Strasse 150, 10999 Berlin, Germany

Zabriskie
maintains a
unique focus
on nature and
culture.

Named after Michelangelo Antonioni's 1970 movie *Zabriskie Point*, Berlin's Zabriskie — Buchladen für Kultur und Natur is a highly specialized store focusing on English and German books and magazines exploring culture and nature. Every book in the store is loved by the booksellers, and you'll find titles on natural history, gardening and self-sufficiency alongside books about underground movies, consciousness, countercultural movements and occult phenomena, amongst other distinctive topics. The mint-hued and sun-filled space in Berlin's Kreuzberg district hosts book presentations and reading groups, and visitors can also shop posters, beautifully designed calendars and a selection of vinyl and tapes.

109   ATLANTIS BOOKS

Nomikos Street, Oía 847 02, Greece

You can browse books while gazing out at the vivid blue Aegean Sea.

Whether you're on your way to take in one of Oía's famous sunsets or you're just looking to escape the afternoon heat, no trip to Santorini is complete without a visit to Atlantis Books. The store was the brainchild of a pair of university students who visited the island and noticed that it lacked a bookstore. They returned after graduation and opened Atlantis Books in 2004. Now located in a white-washed villa, the charming store is packed with new and used books in multiple languages, as well as rare volumes and first editions. The roof terrace is stocked with shelves of used books and offers stunning views of the Santorini caldera.

110   LEXIKOPOLEIO

Stasinou 13, Athens 11635, Greece

TO VISIT
BEFORE YOU DIE
BECAUSE

The Athens
bookstore is a
treasure trove for
language lovers.

Nestled in Athens' historic Kallimarmaro neighborhood is Lexikopoleio, an international bookstore whose name derives from the Greek words for "dictionary" and "to sell." It's a fitting name as the store specializes in languages, offering a large variety of reference, science, humanities and language dictionaries, as well as shelves filled with literature, children's books and comics in Greek, French, English, Italian, German and Spanish. Peruse the two-level store, and if for some reason they don't have the dictionary of your dreams, the friendly staff can special-order it for you.

111 THE OLD BOOKSTORE IN FLATEYRI

Hafnarstræti 3, 425 Flateyri, Iceland

Entering the oldest store in Iceland is like visiting a shoppable museum.

Gamla Bókabúðin á Flateyri, or the Old Bookstore in Flateyri, is a time capsule of a bookstore in Iceland's Westfjords. The store has been run by the same family since it opened in 1914, and other than the updates to the items it sells, it has remained largely untouched. Shoppers can visit the original apartment of the owner and his wife—who lived there from 1915-1950—which has been preserved, and the store operates a guest house upstairs for customers who want to stay awhile. Secondhand books are sold by weight, and the store also carries new books, local products and finds from around the world.

112   HODGES FIGGIS

56-58 Dawson Street, Dublin 2, Ireland

The historic bookstore is a Dublin institution beloved by readers and writers.

The first location of Hodges Figgis opened in 1768, and since then it has become a Dublin institution. This historic company is beloved by both shoppers and writers, even garnering a mention in James Joyce's *Ulysses* and, more recently, in Sally Rooney's *Conversations with Friends*. The store is now set on Dawson Street in a beautiful red-brick Georgian building with four floors of titles and Irish literary greats adorning the walls. Hodges Figgis offers a comprehensive selection of books relating to Ireland, from poetry and fiction to history and nature, alongside volumes of all genres and an academic section.

waterstones.com/bookshops/hodges-figgis   00353 1 677 4754

113   LIBRERIA PALAZZO ROBERTI

Via Jacopo Da Ponte, 34 36061 Bassano del Grappa, Italy

As locations go, it's hard to beat that of Libreria Palazzo Roberti, which is set in a 17th-century noble palace in Bassano del Grappa. The independent bookstore is owned by the Manfrotto family, who restored the Palazzo and opened the store in 1998, and is managed by three sisters: Lavinia, Lorenza and Veronica Manfrotto. Shoppers can explore the building's three floors, with books displayed on the first floor and the mezzanine. The grand hall on the Noble Floor features immaculately restored frescos and is an awe-inspiring location for the store's frequent events, including photography exhibitions, classical concerts and book launches.

114 LIBRERIA ACQUA ALTA

Calle Longa Santa Maria Formosa 5176b, 30122 Venice, Italy

You can browse books stored in bathtubs and a gondola, then take in views of the city's famous canals.

Libreria Acqua Alta, which translates to "high water bookstore," is a unique and whimsical bookstore in Venice, Italy. The store is packed with books—and several cats—and customers can browse the eclectic selection of new and used volumes, magazines and ephemera, which are protected from high tides thanks to being stored in bathtubs, waterproof bins and even a gondola. Climb the staircase of books on the back porch to take in views of the canal, and in case of an emergency, you can take the fire exit: a cheekily labeled door leading straight into the water.

No Website   +39 041 296 0841

115 ANTICA LIBRERIA CASCIANELLI

Largo Febo 14/16, Rome 00186, Italy

The 19th-century store is a cabinet of curiosities filled with unique treasures.

Stepping into Rome's Antica Libreria Cascianelli feels like entering the carefully curated library of an early 19th-century scholar. The bookstore, adjacent to the Piazza Navona, has remained unchanged since the early 1800s, and is filled with treasures galore, including rare books, prints and objets d'art. Valentina La Rocca, Alessandro Lancia and Alfio Mazza have managed the store since 2014 and are responsible for the captivating selection. Browse beautiful volumes set in the original boiserie and blown-glass bookcases, take a peek at the scientific and decorative objects on display in the counters, and don't miss every mystery reader's dream: a secret bookcase door leading to a backroom.

116   LIBRERIA BRAC

Via dei Vagellai, 18/R, 50122 Florence, Italy

TO VISIT
BEFORE YOU DIE
BECAUSE

The bookstore/
restaurant hybrid
nourishes the
mind and the
body.

Part bookstore, part restaurant, Libreria Brac in Florence combines the passions of its owners—a chef specializing in vegetarian and vegan food and a bibliophile devoted to the arts—in a beautiful setting with vaulted ceilings and a scenic courtyard draped with a colorful installation of over 5,000 fabric strips. Shoppers can find a large selection of books on contemporary art, dance, photography, architecture, theater and graphic design in the bright and airy space. Be sure to make a reservation to enjoy a freshly prepared meal made with local and seasonal ingredients and paired with a selection of natural wines.

117 LIBRERIA INTERNAZIONALE LUXEMBURG

Via Cesare Battisti 7, Turin 10123, Italy

TO VISIT
BEFORE YOU DIE
BECAUSE

Argentine newspaper *Clarín* declared it one of the 10 most beautiful bookstores in the world.

For over 150 years, Turin residents have headed to Piazza Carignano to find their next read. Founded in 1872 and originally named Libreria Casanova, the corner store is now the home of Libreria Luxemburg, an international bookstore. The store is packed with books, and shoppers will find well-stocked sections of LGBTQIA+ and Judaica books. Expats and travelers can find international newspapers and magazines at the first-floor newsstand. Climb the creaky wooden stairs to the second floor, where you'll find books in an array of languages, including English, Spanish, French and German.

118 LAFELTRINELLI

Punta Helbronner, Monte Bianco, 11013, Italy

Shop from the top of the world in the highest bookstore in Europe.

In 2019, bookstore chain laFeltrinelli opened its most unusual location: a bookstore on top of a mountain. Set inside the Punta Helbronner/The Sky, the third station on the Skyway Monte Bianco cableway, laFeltrinelli 3466 is located at an altitude of 11,371 feet (3,466 meters). Visitors can enjoy the epic view on their way to the station, then take in the snowy panoramas from the store's floor-to-ceiling windows. The store stocks a small, well-curated selection of 376 titles covering subjects from mountain photography and local cuisine to regional nature and children's books.

119 BOEKHANDEL DEN BOER

Laanstraat 67-69, 3743 BC Baarn, Netherlands

Boekhandel Den Boer was named the most beautiful bookstore in the Netherlands.

This iconic bookstore in Baarn has been a much loved destination since it opened in 1887. The building, which became Boekhandel Den Boer in 1900 and was renovated in 1905 in the Art Nouveau style, maintains its historic beauty with a graceful stone façade, gorgeous woodwork and cabinetry, skylights and original tilework. The store stocks books for all ages, and the friendly staff can help point shoppers to the perfect book. Boekhandel Den Boer organizes frequent events and boasts artistic window displays that are almost as eye-catching as the store itself.

denboer.nl   033-2532300

120 BOEKHANDEL DOMINICANEN

Dominicanerkerkstraat 1, 6211 CZ Maastricht, Netherlands

You can climb the steel walk-in bookcase and take in the spectacular Gothic architecture.

A 13th-century Gothic church in Maastricht is now the home of the stunning Boekhandel Dominicanen. The carefully restored building was outfitted with a massive multi-level walk-in bookcase, which emphasizes the height of the soaring space, holds thousands of books and provides bird's-eye views of the incredible architectural details, such as stone vaults, stained-glass windows, fragments of frescos dating to the early 1600s and a painting of Thomas Aquinas from 1337. The former choir of the Dominican church is a branch of Maastricht coffee roaster Blanche Dael Coffeelovers that also serves as an event space.

boekhandeldominicanen.nl   +31 043 410 00 10

121 BOEKHANDEL BLOKKER

Binnenweg 138, 2101 JP Heemstede, Netherlands

**TO VISIT
BEFORE YOU DIE
BECAUSE**

The whimsical store will delight customers of all ages.

Boekhandel Blokker is a small but charming bookstore that's been a fixture in the North Holland province town of Heemstede for over 60 years. Stop in to browse new releases and bestsellers, including fiction, children's titles and non-fiction, in the mint-hued store, which is decorated with graphic black-and-white checkered floors and whimsical hot-air balloon lighting fixtures. The playful environment makes shopping a delight for all ages, and for readers looking to hear from their favorite authors, the store hosts frequent book launches and interviews with writers.

boekhandelblokker.nl 023-5282472

122 VAN DER VELDE IN DE BROEREN

Achter de Broeren 1-3, 8011 VA Zwolle, Netherlands

The impressive vaults, stained glass and organ in Van der Velde In de Broeren are must-sees.

Built from 1466-1512 by the Domincans, the Broerenkerk in Zwolle passed from owner to owner for nearly 500 years and eventually fell into disrepair, until it was given new life and transformed into a bookstore in 2013. Gaze up at the incredible painted vaults, which date to the 16th century, and climb up to the upper levels of Van der Velde In de Broeren to get an even closer look. Mystery fans will be intrigued by the ancient cold case that was discovered in the church's crypts and can see a replica of the human skeleton, named Herman, that archeologists unearthed in 2010. Try to plan your visit around the organ concerts to hear the church's wonderfully preserved 19th-century organ.

vanderveldeindebroeren.nl   (038) 4215392

123 SCHELTEMA

Rokin 9, 1012 KK Amsterdam, Netherlands

It's one of the largest bookstores in the Netherlands, so it's sure to have just what you're looking for.

Scheltema has been an Amsterdam institution since 1853. In 2015, it moved to its current location in the Rokin area, and is a massive store offering over 125,000 titles across five floors and over 34,000 square feet of retail space. The long-established bookseller offers new and secondhand books, hosts hundreds of events each year, and even boasts a fully functional kitchen where chefs and cookbook authors such as Jamie Oliver and Yotam Ottolenghi have conducted cooking demonstrations. A Vascabelo Café-Brasserie is located on the second floor should you get hungry after surveying the sizable store.

124 TRONSMO BOKHANDEL

Universitetsgata 12, 0164 Oslo, Norway

TO VISIT
BEFORE YOU DIE
BECAUSE

American poet Allen Ginsberg called Tronsmo Bokhandel the best bookstore in the world.

The Oslo bookstore has left a lasting impression on its many customers since it was founded in 1973. Tronsmo is an independent bookstore with an independent spirit. Its inventory is made up of books the owners feel deserve attention, including volumes on globalization and politics and also on photography. Beat literature, crime novels and LGBTQIA+ books are also specialisms. The basement is home to the legendary comics section, which features an incredible selection of classic, indie and underground series from around the world.

125 LIVRARIA DE SANTIAGO

Largo de São Tiago do Castelo, 2510-006 Óbidos, Portugal

This beautiful bookstore is set in a UNESCO City of Literature.

A 12th-century church was converted into Livraria de Santiago, a stunning bookstore in the medieval walled city of Óbidos, which was named a UNESCO City of Literature in 2015. A curved wooden structure winds through the store displaying a selection of books in Portuguese, as well as a few in English. Architectural details, which date to when the church was rebuilt in 1772 following an earthquake, can be seen throughout, including the altar, stone accents and marble floors. The store plays host to frequent film screenings, exhibitions and book launches.

No Website +351 939 079 707

126 LIVRARIA LELLO

Rua das Carmelitas, 144, 4050-161 Porto, Portugal

TO VISIT
BEFORE YOU DIE
BECAUSE

Browsing the shelves of this Porto landmark feels like stepping back in time.

One of the oldest bookstores in Portugal, Livraria Lello is set in a 1906 Neo-Gothic building, home to stunning architectural details, such as an iconic center staircase, stained-glass ceiling and intricately carved arches. Readers can browse the extensive selection of classics, visit the wonderful Little Prince's room, see the mirror box with the Bob Dylan's love letters or make an appointment to access GEMMA, the recently opened rare book room, where Jim Morrison's personal copy of the first edition of *Moby Dick*, a signed and numbered copy of the first edition of *The Picture of Dorian Gray* and a signed first edition of *Harry Potter and the Philosopher's Stone* are on display. The bookstore is such an attraction that entrance vouchers must be purchased in order to visit.

127   LIVRARIA ALMEDINA RATO

Rua da Escola Politécnica No 225, 1250-101 Lisbon, Portugal

The store offers literature in a setting that offers a glimpse of Lisbon history.

Joaquim Machado founded the first branch of Livraria Almedina in 1955, and since then the company has grown to include 11 stores. Almedina Rato, which opened in 2017, is set in a historic building that used to serve as the workshop of Ricardo Leone, a famed stained-glass and mosaic artist. After entering through the traditional blue-and-white tile-framed doorway, shoppers can get a sense of the building's rich history through the many original elements that have been preserved, such as the glass cutting tables which are now topped with books. Art fans can check out the selection of volumes fittingly located in Leone's former office.

128   CARTURESTI CARUSEL

Strada Lipscani 55, Bucharest 030033, Romania

This historic building has been given a stunning new life as a world-class bookstore.

Cărturești Carusel is set in a spectacular 19th-century building in the old city center of Bucharest. The building was purchased in 1903 by Greek bankers, the Chrissoveloni family, but was confiscated by the Communist regime in the 1950s. After years of being used as a clothing store, the building fell into disrepair. It was recovered and rejuvenated by Jean Chrissoveloni, a descendant of the former owners, who opened the six-level bookstore, which houses over 10,000 volumes and 5,000 movies and albums. Shoppers can grab a bite at the bistro on the top floor, visit the multimedia space in the basement and explore the contemporary art gallery on the main level.

129 PODPISNIE IZDANIYA

Liteiny Avenue 57, St. Petersburg 191014, Russia

Podpisnie Izdaniya has been selling books in St. Petersburg since 1926, and prides itself on combining traditions of the city's book trade with modern European trends. It settled in its current home in 1958, a stylish and sunny multi-level store. Colorful tiles line the floors and soaring bookshelves equipped with rolling library ladders line the double-height spaces. Find a book from the store's wide selection of titles including intellectual literature and a comprehensive art history section, then grab a coffee or a glass of wine from one of the two cafés. Don't miss the stationery, which the company produces in collaboration with contemporary designers and illustrators.

130 JEWISH MUSEUM SHOP

Obraztsova Street 11, Building 1A, Moscow, Russia

The bookstore in the Jewish Museum and Tolerance Center in Moscow is a beautiful space to learn and reflect. The museum is located in an incredible brick space designed in 1926 by Russian avant-garde architect Konstantin Melnikov. The shop was renovated in 2019 by the firm Architectural buro A2M, who call their concept the "endless bookstore." A 59-foot-long (and book-topped) copper counter spans the space and separates the bookstore from the exhibition area, while the 16-foot-tall bookcases recall classical libraries and feature rolling ladders for hard-to-reach titles. Readers can find volumes of literature alongside the work of Israeli authors, art books, memoirs and rare editions.

131 TYPEWRONGER BOOKS

4a Haddington Place, Edinburgh EH7 4AE, Scotland

As a bookstore and typewriter repair shop, Typewronger is a destination for both readers and writers. Shoppers descend a flight of stairs to reach the petite store, which is Edinburgh's smallest bookstore and a hidden gem in the city. Find volumes of poetry in the quaint poetry nook, as well as a curated selection of books throughout the store. Customers are encouraged to use the Royal 10 typewriter on the main desk (you can bring your own paper or use theirs), and the store is open late—9 p.m. Sunday-Friday and 10 p.m. on Saturdays—for all your evening reading needs.

132 DESPERATE LITERATURE

Calle Campomanes, 13, 28013 Madrid, Spain

Desperate Literature celebrates secondhand books and up-and-coming authors.

If you want to know what the cool kids are reading these days, head to Desperate Literature, an international bookstore in Madrid brought to you by Craig Walzer, Corey Eastwood, Charlotte Delattre and Terry Craven, the booksellers behind Atlantis Books in Santorini, and Book Thug Nation and Human Relations in Brooklyn. The well-stocked location carries used books for adults and children in English, Spanish, French and other languages. The focus is on fiction, sci-fi, poetry and noir, but you'll also find books on a range of different topics, from philosophy to film. Desperate Literature also offers an annual short fiction prize celebrating unpublished fiction under 2,000 words.

133   LA BIBLIOTECA DE BABEL

Carrer Arabí 3, 07003 Palma, Mallorca, Spain

What could
be better than
browsing books,
then enjoying a
glass of wine?

Bibliophiles and vinophiles will both love La Biblioteca de Babel, a bookstore in Palma, Mallorca. The store, whose name is a nod to the book by Jorge Luis Borges, is set in an old building behind the Basilica de Sant Miguel de Palma. Shoppers walk past the charming café tables to enter the bookstore, where a trove of titles is displayed in a cozy setting framed by wood beams. Over 200 wines and a selection of spirits are also on offer at the store's bar, and the staff can recommend the perfect book and a glass of vino to enjoy with it.

labibliotecadebabel.es   971 721 442

134   LLIBRERIA FINESTRES

Diputació, 249, 08007 Barcelona, Spain

Llibreria Finestres describes itself as a bookstore for reading, and it is indeed a place you'll want to linger with a good book. The beautifully decorated store opened in 2021 and offers books in Spanish and Catalan, as well as titles in other languages, including English, French, Portuguese, Basque and Galician. Once you find a book, you can while away the day reading on the velvet sofas or over a glass of wine in the café and bar. Directly across the street you'll find the equally beautiful Finestres 250, which is dedicated to books on art, cinema, music, comics and more.

llibreriafinestres.com   93 384 08 09

135 LIBRERÍA MIGUEL MIRANDA

Calle Lope de Vega, 19, Madrid 28014, Spain

Librería Miguel Miranda is a collection of treasures in a spectacular setting.

Librería Miguel Miranda is everything you would expect from an antiquarian bookstore. Founded in 1949 by actor-turned-bookseller Miguel Miranda Vicente on Madrid's Paseo del Prado, the family-owned store is now run by the third generation and is located in a dazzling home in the city's Literary Quarter. Book-filled cabinets line the walls and an ornate spiral staircase leads to the mezzanine, where more books and architectural details await. You'll find a robust selection of antique volumes and affordable out-of-print books covering an array of topics from anthropology to zoology within the elegant space.

libreriamiranda.com   (+34) 914 294 576

136 TIPOS INFAMES

Calle San Joaquin 3, 28004 Madrid, Spain

TO VISIT
BEFORE YOU DIE
BECAUSE

You can sip and shop at this bookstore dedicated to independent publishers and authors.

Sip a glass of rioja as you peruse the shelves at Tipos Infames in Madrid's Malasaña neighborhood. The store, which opened in 2010, specializes in literature from independent publishers and authors, which you can pair with a glass of wine or a craft beer from the wine bar or a cappuccino from the café. Tipos Infames was also founded to be a destination for all types of culture, with frequent events such as exhibitions, book presentations and wine tastings. In 2019, the store expanded across the street with a new space dedicated to poetry, graphic novels and books for children and young adults.

137 NEVER STOP READING

Spiegelgasse 18, 8001 Zürich, Switzerland

TO VISIT
BEFORE YOU DIE
BECAUSE

The store housed in a former butcher shop has an excellent selection of architecture, photography and art books.

Located in Zürich's old town, Never Stop Reading is a must-visit bookstore on Spiegelgasse, one of the city's most famous streets and the former home of author Georg Büchner and the Dada art movement. The bookstore is set in a space that once housed a butcher shop, and remnants of its past life, including tile walls, remain. Shoppers will find a wide range of international titles focused on art, design, architecture and photography and can browse the frequent art exhibitions on display. Never Stop Reading is a partner bookstore with Büchergilde Gutenberg and has a section of fiction and non-fiction from the German publishing cooperative.

138 THE BOOK CELLAR

132 High Street, Campbell Town, Tasmania 7210, Australia

TO VISIT
BEFORE YOU DIE
BECAUSE

You'll find a
large selection
of Tasmanian
books in a unique,
historic setting.

Tasmania's The Book Cellar boasts thousands of new and used books in a historical setting. The bookshop is located in The Foxhunters Return, a Georgian coaching inn built in the 1830s. The cellars, which now house the bookshop, once were home to the convict workers who built the Red Bridge over the Elizabeth River. (These prisoners are memorialized on the Convict Brick Trail, which begins just outside the building.) The brick-and-stone walled store offers a diverse selection of books, including an extensive list of new, out-of-print and antiquarian Tasmanian titles as well as volumes on hunting and fishing and regions such as Antarctica, the Pacific Islands and New Zealand.

139   BOOKSHOP BY URO

5/30 Perry Street, Collingwood, VIC 3066, Australia

Architecture
and design fans
will enjoy the
minimalist shop
and its inventory.

Find an immaculately curated selection of art, architecture and design books at Bookshop by Uro in Collingwood Yards, an arts precinct in Melbourne's inner north. The shop is owned and managed by Uro Publications and is set in a minimalist space designed by the firm Architecture architecture, which installed warm wood cantilevered shelves, a long timber bench and mirrored surfaces to help the room feel larger. The shop hosts frequent exhibitions, book launches and discussions in the flexible space. Peruse titles on everything from landscape design to urbanism, including volumes published by Uro, and be sure to visit the restored Keith Haring mural nearby.

140 TITLE BOOKS BARANGAROO

400 Barangaroo Avenue, Barangaroo NSW 2000, Australia

There's something for everyone, whether you're a book lover, music fan or movie buff.

Cinephiles, audiophiles and bibliophiles will all find something to enjoy (and take home) at TITLE Books Barangaroo, an independent bookstore set in a strikingly modern building in the Barangaroo area of Sydney. The company's slogan "TITLE is not about what's new, it's about what's great," rings true from the moment you start to browse the store. You can find an array of books ranging from fiction to coffee table books on fashion, design and architecture, along with CDs, new and classic vinyl albums and movies, including Japanese, French and Italian cinema. The expert staff are there to help point you to the exact book, movie or album you never knew you needed but now can't live without.

141   GERTRUDE & ALICE

46 Hall Street, Bondi Beach, NSW 2026, Australia

TO VISIT
BEFORE YOU DIE
BECAUSE

The Bondi Beach store is a book lover's heaven inspired by literary greats.

Named after ex-pat authors Gertrude Stein and Alice B. Toklas, Gertrude & Alice Bookstore & Coffee Shop is an independent bookstore located in a former surf shop in Bondi Beach. Founders Jane Turner and Katerina Cosgrove were inspired by everything from Turkish antiquarian bookstores, Moroccan tea rooms and Paris's Shakespeare and Company bookshop when coming up with the idea for the store over 20 years ago. They wanted it to be a literary haven and have created just that. The store offers new, antiquarian and vintage books, which are displayed from floor to ceiling in the delightfully packed space.

142 POTTS POINT BOOKSHOP

14 Macleay Street, Potts Point, Elizabeth Bay,
NSW 2011, Australia

TO VISIT
BEFORE YOU DIE
BECAUSE

The award-winning
booksellers at the
inviting community
bookstore
give expert
recommendations.

Award-winning independent bookseller Potts Point Bookshop is a
warm and welcoming spot in Elizabeth Bay. Customers are greeted
by an elegant entry with chevron floors and a center table piled
high with new releases and a dramatic floral arrangement. Floor-
to-ceiling wooden bookcases line the walls of the shop and con-
tain carefully selected titles in all genres. Young readers will find
everything from board books to young adult fiction. The experi-
enced and knowledgeable staff are on hand to make recommendations and the store hosts two book clubs each month, where guests
enjoy lively discussions about that month's title.

pottspointbookshop.com.au   +61 2 9331 6642

143 BERKELOUW BOOK BARN

Bendooley Estate, 3020 Old Hume Highway, Berrima, NSW 2577, Australia

The Berkelouw family first began selling books in Rotterdam in 1812. Following the destruction of its entire inventory during World War II, the company established itself in Australia, where it is now the country's largest bookseller. You can find its most captivating location on the Bendooley Estate, where it operates Berkelouw Book Barn. Thousands of new and secondhand titles are housed in the picturesque and cavernous barn, which features a large stone fireplace and iron chandeliers, and also hosts the estate's restaurant and bar. The company's rare book section can be found in a second barn right down the lane.

berkelouw.com.au   (02) 4868 8700

144 READINGS EMPORIUM

Woiworung Country, Emporium Melbourne, Shop 1-016/287 Lonsdale Street, Melbourne, VIC 3000, Australia

While independent bookseller Readings has a number of locations in Melbourne, its eighth store, which opened in 2022 in the Emporium Melbourne complex, might be its loveliest. Kerstin Thompson Architects were the creative minds behind the striking, light-filled space, which was designed to encourage browsing and offer a quiet retreat from the busy shopping center outside. The store houses over 1,000 feet of bookshelves, and customers will find seating areas beside the huge arched windows that overlook Little Bourke Street. The children's section is decorated with a colorful mural painted by illustrator Kat Macleod, and the tall center aisle is the perfect spot to get lost for a while.

145   AMPERSAND CAFE & BOOKSTORE

78 Oxford Street, Paddington, NSW 2021, Australia

You can work up an appetite browsing over 30,000 books, then enjoy a gourmet meal in the café.

Located in Paddington, Ampersand Café & Bookstore offers delicious dining and a vast selection of over 30,000 secondhand books. Booklovers can browse the three floors of unique volumes, including biographies, literature, travel writing, art monographs and a selection of collectible books. Find a cozy corner (there are many) and peruse your finds. If you get hungry from flipping through books, grab a seat in the café or the adjacent laneway and enjoy a coffee or a full meal from the mouthwatering menu of breakfast, brunch and lunch dishes.

146 HORDERN HOUSE

2/255 Riley Street, Surry Hills, Sydney, NSW 2010, Australia

Hordern House offers one-of-a-kind treasures in a chic warehouse space.

Browse an exquisite collection of rare books, manuscripts, maps and objects in a stunning setting at Hordern House in Sydney. The renowned dealer operates out of a beautifully decorated floor of a converted warehouse in Surry Hills and specializes in books and materials on voyages and travel, particularly items related to Australia and the Pacific. Booklovers will delight in volumes from the 18th, 19th and early 20th centuries as well as illustrated leaves from the 1400s. The store is open by appointment only, so be sure to call or email to schedule your visit.

hordern.com (+61) 02 9356 4411

147 GRAND DAYS

220 William Street, Woolloomooloo, NSW 2011, Australia

TO VISIT
BEFORE YOU DIE
BECAUSE

You can shop secondhand books and vintage fashion at this unique Woolloomooloo store.

Update your bookshelves and your wardrobe all in one place at this standout Woolloomooloo store. Owners Tamara Kennedy and Tom Hespe took over the store (formerly Bedgen's Books) in 2013 and created an emporium of vintage treasures, which they named Grand Days in homage to the book by Frank Moorhouse and its eccentric main character Edith Campbell Berry. The vintage emporium is home to an array of books, including Australian literature, classics, art and architecture titles, poetry and plays. You'll also find other pre-loved collectibles, such as records, designer fashion and accessories in the boutique-like space.

148 THE NEXT CHAPTER

72 Brownston Street, Wānaka 9305, New Zealand

TO VISIT
BEFORE YOU DIE
BECAUSE

Each book in the
small store has
earned a place on
the shelves.

While it may occupy a small footprint, The Next Chapter in Wānaka has big bookstore energy. Owners Jenny Ainge and Sally Battson opened their independent bookstore in a shipping-container–style space in 2020, bringing a much needed resource to Southern Lakes residents. The pair carefully choose each book on the shelves, offering fiction and non-fiction titles from New Zealand and international authors, including children's books and an outdoor and mountaineering section. The Next Chapter is located beside Cinema Paradiso, and the two businesses collaborate on events in the covered courtyard, including author lectures and book clubs.

      nextchapterwanaka.co.nz   +64 (0)21 090 46330

149 PETRONELLA'S GALLERY AND BOOKSTORE

Shop 8, Rapuwai Lane, SH 8 Lake Tekapo 7945, New Zealand

TO VISIT
BEFORE YOU DIE
BECAUSE

The welcoming store carries an excellent selection of books by New Zealand authors.

Petronella's Gallery and Bookstore in Lake Tekapo describes itself as an independent bookstore with an independent spirit. In 2018, owner Wilma van den Bosch first opened the store in two garages, and in 2020, the store moved to its current location in the town center. Van den Bosch stocks books in a wide variety of genres from modern fiction to gardening, fishing and cooking titles. Find fiction, photography and non-fiction volumes by New Zealand authors as well as plenty of finds for young readers.

150   BROWSERS

Riverbank Lane, 298 Victoria Street, Hamilton 3204, New Zealand

TO VISIT
BEFORE YOU DIE
BECAUSE

The two-story bookcase is a sight to behold at this well-stocked store.

Browsers is a paradise of secondhand books in Hamilton. Rachel Pope opened the store in 1996, making her bookstore ownership dream a reality, and since then, the store has become a beloved part of the community. A towering two-story bookcase makes an great first impression on customers, who should prepare to spend hours getting lost in the huge collection of titles, including some first editions and signed volumes. The charming children's section has a reading nook for the store's young customers to curl up in with a picture book or two.

Index 150 Bookstores

© Photos

In the same series

150 Bars You Need to
Visit Before You Die
ISBN 9789401486194

150 Hotels
You Need to Visit
Before You Die
ISBN 9789401458061

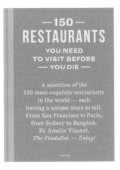

150 Restaurants
You Need to Visit
Before You Die
ISBN 9789401454421

150 Houses
You Need to Visit
Before You Die
ISBN 9789401462044

150 Gardens You Need
to Visit Before You Die
ISBN 9789401479295

150 Golf Courses You
Need to Visit Before
You Die
ISBN 9789401481953

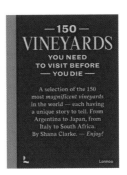

150 Vineyards
You Need to Visit
Before You Die
ISBN 9789401485463

Colophon

Texts
Elizabeth Stamp

Copy-editing
Melanie Shapiro

Book Design
ASB

Sign up for our newsletter with news about new
and forthcoming publications on art, interior
design, food & travel, photography and fashion
as well as exclusive offers and events. If you have
any questions or comments about the material in
this book, please do not hesitate to contact our
editorial team: art@lannoo.com

© Lannoo Publishers, Belgium, 2023
D/2023/45/172 - NUR450/500
ISBN 978 94 014 8935 5
2nd print run

www.lannoo.com